birth reborn

introduction by sheila kitzinger

translated by jane pincus and juliette levin

birth reborn

Dr. michel odent

SOUVENIR PRESS

First published in the United States by Pantheon Books, a division of
Random House, Inc., New York, and simultaneously in Canada by
Random House of Canada Limited, Toronto.
From an unpublished French manuscript by Michel Odent.
Copyright © as an unpublished work, 1984 by Michel Odent.
Parts of Sheila Kitzinger's introduction have previously appeared in
Good Housekeeping (U.K.)
First British edition (hardback) published 1984 by
Souvenir Press Ltd., 43 Great Russell Street, London WCIB 3PA.

Special thanks to Suzanne Arms for photographic consultation.
Photos on pages 3, 4, 7, 17, 20, 21, 28, 3 1, 37, 43, 45, 47 (bottom), 60, 61,
64, 68, 69, 70, 71, 78 (top) 79, 83, 92, 93, 115, 116, 119 © Suzanne Arms.
Photos on pages 9, 12, 13, 29, 38, 39, 42, 47 (top) 50, 51, 52, 54, 55, 57, 58, 59, 62,
63, 65, 67, 74, 77, 87, 99, 104, 105, 107, 109, 110, 111, 112 © Dominique Pourré.
Photos on pages 2, 19, 23, 24, 25, 80, 81, 114 © Pascale L. R.
Photos on pages 14, 15, 48, 49,78 (bottom) © Lyu Hanabusa.
Photo on page 10 © Michel Odent
Photos on pages 22, 40, 76, 89 © H. Vernay and N. Heinimann.
Photo on page 27 © Georges Melet.
Photos on pages 72, 73 © Jacques-Marie Le Roux.

Second edition (paperback) 1994
Reprinted 2005 (with new introduction)
Reprinted 2008, 2013

ISBN 978 0 285 63194 6

Printed and bound in India by Replika Press Pvt. Ltd.

to my mother, for her eighty-eighth birthday

I want to thank Sara Bershtel of Pantheon Books
and Jane Pincus, who convinced me to write such a book
and who gave me much precious advice.

contents

introduction (2005 reprint) | xi
introduction (first edition) | xvii
introduction to the Second Edition | xxv
pithiviers | 3
before | 21
helping women in labor | 39
the first hour and after | 6
anti-obstetrics | 93
birth reborn | 115

notes | 121

introduction

2005 REPRINT

1984, 1994, 2005...In the middle of every decade we feel the need to introduce or reintroduce *Birth Reborn* in an evolving context. Perhaps, one day, this succession of introductions will appear as an overview of the history of childbirth in relation to the evolution of our civilizations.

The 1994 introduction focused on the advent of "evidence based" midwifery and obstetrics. The practices we had developed in a French state hospital during the 1970s and early 1980s were mostly based on personal experience and intuition: when the second edition was published most of them were supported by scientific evaluations. For example we were originally in trouble to explain our reluctance to record the baby's heartbeat during labour with an electronic machine. We just intuitively guessed that when a laboring woman knows that her body functions are continuously monitored, her neocortex (the thinking brain) is stimulated; the main effect would therefore be to make the birth longer, more difficult and therefore more dangerous. With the advent of evidence-based obstetrics, dozens of studies confirmed that the only constant and significant effects on statistics of electronic fetal monitoring —compared with intermittent auscultation— was to increase the rates of caesareans.

Since the 1994 edition the history of childbirth is led in two opposite directions by two groups of events. The first group of events is directly related to obstetrics. A combination of technical advances made caesarean birth so safe that it is now considered a common way to be born. It is likely that in the near future many cities and even countries all over the world will pass the 50 per cent mark. This long list includes the majority of Latin America and a great part of the Asian continent: India, China, Taiwan, Singapore and South Korea. It also includes several Southern European countries. At the dawn of the new century we can understand those who claim that the caesarean will soon be the usual way to give birth. We can understand, for example, the point of view of an influential professor of obstetrics who anticipates that in the future the unpredictable risks of labour will no longer be justified for most women.[1] We can understand why many female obstetricians with an uncomplicated pregnancy at term would choose a scheduled caesarean delivery for the birth of their own baby.[2] We can also understand the conclusions of authoritative committees who consider it ethical to offer all pregnant women an elective caesarean.

Until now the practices of midwifery and obstetrics have been evaluated through conventional "twentieth-century criteria".[3] These include the number of babies alive and healthy at birth, the frequency of maternal health problems, maternal satisfaction and cost effectiveness. According to these sole criteria the safety of the caesarean is comparable to the safety of the vaginal route in well-equipped and well-organized departments of obstetrics. There are therefore serious reasons to conclude that caesareans are the future.

The second group of events is not directly related to childbirth and obstetrics. Today a great variety of scientific disciplines provide data that prompt us to think long term and to think in terms of civilization. They introduce new concepts that should become the basis of the "twenty-first century criteria" for evaluating how babies are born. These new concepts reinforce the intuitive knowledge shared by a great number of women (and even men) who feel that we should reverse the current tendencies urgently.

This second group of events includes what I have called "The scientification of love".[4] Until recently, love was the realm of poets, novelists and philosophers. Today it is studied from a variety of scientific perspectives. All scientific data converge to give a great importance to early experiences, particularly to the period surrounding birth. They suggest simple and paradoxically new questions, such as: how does the capacity to love develop? During these past ten years, we have dramatically improved our knowledge of the behavioural effects of hormones involved in childbirth and other episodes of our sexual life. We can use this developing field of research to explain why the history of childbirth is really at a crossroad. The flow of hormones that mammals in general—and humans in particular—are supposed to release to give birth is a cocktail of "love hormones". For millions of years our female ancestors could not give birth and deliver the placenta without releasing this complex mixture of hormones, which includes oxytocin, considered the typical "love hormone". Today, in our societies, most women have babies without relying on the effects of their natural hormones. Many have a caesarean. Those who give birth by the vaginal route often use drugs that block the release of the natural hormones and don't have their behavioural effects. For example, an intravenous drip of synthetic oxytocin blocks the release of the natural main love hormone, is effective at stimulating uterine contractions, but does not reach the brain and has no behavioural effects. This is an unprecedented situation. What is the future of civilization if women have babies without releasing such a hormonal cocktail? Where human beings are concerned we must always think in terms of civilization, while among non-human mammals the behavioural effects of disturbing the birth process are detectable at an individual level: when ewes, for example, give birth with an epidural anaeshesia, they simply don't take care of their lamb.

Among the disciplines that participate in the "scientification of love", we must mention "Primal Health Research". This new generation of research includes studies that explore the links between the "primal period" and health and behaviour later on in life. According to the interpretation I proposed for this term in the past,[5] the "primal period" goes from conception until the first birthday. The development of Primal Health Research is increasing, to such a point that our research centre—the Primal Health Research Centre—has established and is constantly updating a database with hundreds of references of studies published in authoritative scientific and medical journals.[6] From an overview of our data bank it appears that when researchers explore the background of people exhibiting some sort of "impaired capacity to love"—either love of oneself or love of others—they often detect risk factors in the period surrounding birth. Furthermore, when such correlations have been found, it usually concerns topical issues. The concept of "impaired capacity to love", although new, gives rise to a convenient classification system for some major current health preoccupations. Among the key words leading to such studies we must mention in particular violent criminality, suicide, drug addiction, anorexia nervosa and autism. Our data bank can also be presented as a tool to condition ourselves to think long term.

Futuristic strategies

When introducing the "twenty-first century criteria", we bring to light new and vital reasons to disturb the physiological processes as little as possible and to try to reverse the current tendencies. Understanding the lessons of the scientification of love and acquiring the capacity to think long term are the basis for future strategies. The aim should be that as many women as possible give birth relying on an undisturbed flow of love hormones. The main obstacle is a widespread and quasi-cultural lack of understanding of birth physiology. In other words we have to rediscover the basic needs of women in labor. They have been forgotten after thousands of years of culturally controlled childbirth, decades of industrialized childbirth and a proliferation of "methods" of "natural" childbirth (as if the words "method" and "natural" were compatible). All mammals share these basic needs. All mammals need to feel secure when giving birth: they postpone the delivery if there is a predator around. All mammals need privacy: they have strategies not to feel observed during the period surrounding birth. Rediscovering these basic needs will lead to the revival of authentic midwifery. A midwife is a mother figure. In an ideal world our mother is the prototype of the person with whom we feel secure without feeling observed or judged.

It is only when the basic needs of labouring women and the specific role of the midwife are physiologically interpreted that a shift towards new and simple strategies in childbirth will become possible. These strategies will take into account the safety of the modern caesarean. Anyone exploring our data bank will be convinced of the importance of avoiding drugs during labor, of avoiding long and difficult births by the vaginal route and the use of tools such as forceps, of avoiding "non-labor caesareans" and also last minute emergency caesareans (when there is a race between the surgeon and the progress of a fetal distress).

We must therefore prepare for a binary strategy, with two basic scenarios.[6]

Either the birth process is straightforward by the vaginal route. *Or* it is not. The latter scenario should lead to an in-labor, non-emergency caesarean. The critical task is to decide early enough during the first stage of labor when a caesarean is indicated. We need non-pharmacological tests adapted to twenty-first century strategies. The "birthing pool test" is a good example of a tool adapted to futuristic scenarios. It is based on the simple fact that when a woman in hard labor enters the birthing pool and is immersed in water at body temperature, spectacular progress in dilation should occur within an hour or two. If already well-advanced dilation remains stable in spite of water immersion, privacy (no camera!) and dim light, one can conclude that there is probably a major obstacle. There is no reason to procrastinate. It is wiser to perform an in-labor, non-emergency caesarean right away.

Such a simple binary strategy is compatible with both drugless practices and low rates of surgical intervention. It is not an unattainable ideal: this is probably, in retrospect, the main lesson of *Birth Reborn.*

At the dawn of the twenty-first century, we must confront the implications of an easy, safe and well-accepted caesarean with the lessons provided by the "scientification of love".

We must urgently ask the unaskable: Can humanity survive the safe caesarean?

References:

1. Steer, P. (1998), "Caesarean section: an evolving procedure?" *Brit J Obstet Gynecol* 105:1052–55.
2. Al-Mufti, R., McCarthy, A., Fisk, N.M. (1997), Survey of obstetricians' personal preference and discretionary practice. *Eur J Obstet Gynecol Reprod Biol* 73:1–4.
3. Michel Odent (2004), *The Caesarean*. Free Association Books. London 2004.
4. Michel Odent (1999), *The Scientification of Love*. Free Association Books. London.
5. Michel Odent (1986), *Primal Health*. Century Hutchinson. London (second edition Clairview 2002).
6. www.birthworks.org/primalhealth.

introduction
FIRST EDITION

They lie like stranded whales, enormous undulations of flesh, immobilized and trapped on narrow tables under glaring lights. Each of the four women is separated from the next by only a curtain. From between her legs a wire projects. It is linked to a machine with a rapidly flashing green eye, and from this a long strip of ticker-tape is steadily but tidily vomited, falling in thickening folds as time wears on. Another wire, recording uterine pressure, connects with the machine, too, and produces its own eruption of jagged lines. "Lie still," the women are told. "Any movement will interfere with the print-out of the monitor." But it is not possible for them to move. Each has no sensation at all from above her belly down to her feet. Taped to one shoulder is the epidural catheter through which more anaesthetic can be injected when feeling returns. A nurse passes quietly between one woman and the next, checking the machines. A woman asks if she might have a drink; her mouth is very dry. "I am sorry, nothing by mouth." The nurse frowns critically at something on the print-out, and turns to the next machine.

The scene is a West German hospital, but it could be any modern maternity floor, replete with all the high technology that obstetricians are vying with each other to use. I suddenly feel that the women aren't like whales so much as tethered cows in an electronic, space-age milking parlor, taking up the minimum space, making the minimum fuss, the birth of each child managed, processed, measured, and recorded minutely. "It is reassuring," one woman says. "It makes me feel safe." This is the only feeling she describes after her baby is delivered—being safe, and then "relieved" at the birth.

Another woman is in labor, this time in France. She is in a small room in subdued light, with a midwife and her husband close to and supporting her. She is on a low dais that occupies one corner of the room. It is covered with cushions. But she has chosen to squat, with her man behind and holding her. Everything is very quiet. There are no ticking or bleeping machines, no bells ringing; voices are hushed. The usual bustle of a hospital has been blotted out, phones silenced; there are no hurrying feet. This is the maternity unit where Michel Odent works.

Until now this woman paced about, wanting to be upright, pausing only when a contraction came to lean against her husband. But she is starting the second stage of labor and longs to bend her knees and allow the great, heavy weight she feels pressing in her to sink lower, fanning out all the concertina-like folds of her vagina so that it opens wider and wider to help the baby's head pass through.

She is completely enclosed within her experience. Nothing else matters. Nothing intrudes. It is as if she is in her own circle of solitude. She knows exactly what to do and needs no instructions, because she is so completely in tune with her own body and with the energy that is rushing through it in great waves of desire to push the baby down. The midwife waits, hands resting, occasionally whispering, "Good . . . good." Suddenly the woman lets out a long, low moan and there is the top of the baby's head, already born. The midwife still waits. And with the next contraction the woman gives a cry that seems one of astonishment and jubilation and pain and triumph—perhaps also of ecstasy—mingled in one great shout. The baby's head slips through, and then the whole body tumbles out onto the cloth that is spread to receive it. Immediately the mother looks down, scoops up her baby, and lifts it to her breast: "I can't believe it! It's incredible! Don't cry, little one! My baby! My baby! Fantastic! Incredible!" she exclaims over and over again, eyes shining and wet with tears, laughing and crying at the same time. She is in her husband's arms and he is kissing her. Nobody intrudes. He kisses the baby's foot, then his wife again. He is crying with the joy and wonder of it, too. This is what birth is like for some women. This is what birth *can* be.

I first met Michel Odent in 1977, after I had given a paper at an international obstetrical conference. I had said: "The right environment for birth is exactly the same as the environment in which to make love." A note came from him saying: "I agree. Come and see what we are doing at Pithiviers." That year I was busy writing in an old house in the forest of Fontainebleu. The village of Pithiviers was only half an hour's drive away. It was this lucky chance that enabled me to get to know him and to become convinced that women in the United States and in Britain should hear about what he was doing. Here was a man who was no mere obstetric choreographer, but one who shared with women what they experienced themselves and who was on their side.

It is tempting for an obstetrician to become the stage manager of the drama of birth. The "active management" of labor is now very fashionable, and the obstetrician who is successful in the eyes of his colleagues is the one who has the skills to take control of labor and make it conform to a pattern. The woman is passive. She is a physically immobilized patient. Her helplessness is epitomized by the lithotomy position, in which she lies flat on her back with her legs up in stirrups—a posture that is clearly adopted for the convenience and comfort of the obstetrician, not the woman having the baby. Many women find it painful and terrifying to be pushing the baby into thin air as they lie flat on a narrow slab.

Michel Odent provides a setting for birth in which a woman is free to do things *her* way. Anything goes. If she wants to scream, she screams. If she chooses to labor in darkness or to have her other children with her, to walk around or to float in a pool of water, she is encouraged to do any of these things. Most women spontaneously choose to be upright for delivery, their feet firmly planted on the ground, physically supported by doctor, midwife, or labor companion. The baby slides down onto the ground and the mother sees her child immediately, without the need for anyone to hand it to her.

After delivery, too, Michel Odent emphasizes the mother's initiative. In this he differs from Frederic Leboyer, whose teachings inspired him and some of whose methods, like bathing the newborn, he uses at Pithiviers. In a birth film made by Leboyer, the mother is supine; the doctor lifts the baby out and massages it while it lies on her abdomen, or holds the baby isolated from her in the ritual bath. She may reach out her hands, obviously longing to touch her baby; but this is not part of Leboyer's plan. He is focused entirely on the newborn. The relationship between mother and baby is secondary, something that has to come subsequently. In contrast, a woman in Michel Odent's care has an altogether more active role. *She* is the birthgiver. The mother is usually the first to touch her child—it is she who, together with the father, holds the baby ·in a bath set between her legs. In Pithiviers, everybody present at a birth is there to serve and to cherish the woman who is bearing the child.

The point about Michel Odent is that he is ready to learn from women themselves, a rare thing in an obstetrician. He is not yet another man telling women what they should do, another obstetrician giving women instructions about their role in childbirth. Michel Odent speaks with a different voice. He seeks to serve women who want a labor that is a personal, intimate, and deeply creative experience. He offers no magical, quick solution but works to discover an environment for birth in which a woman is, above all, not a patient, or a contracting uterus and a birth canal, or a piece of complicated reproductive machinery, but her *self*.

This usually happens only when a woman gives birth on territory that she herself controls: in her own home, where the doctor—if there is one—and the midwife are *guests*. Certainly it does not usually happen in hospitals. Our Western way of birth has produced many blocks to "doing what comes naturally" and has drained the sexuality from childbirth. Obstetric intervention ranges all the way from routine nursing procedures such as shaving pubic hair and administering enemas or suppositories to artificial rupture of the membranes, oxytocin intravenous drips, electronic monitoring, and drugs that tranquilize, stupefy, disorient, cause hallucinations, produce amnesia, change the woman's body chemistry, and also deprive the fetus of oxygen turning the newborn baby into a limp, sleepy little bundle with a headache, instead of a wide-eyed, searching, learning creature.

Fathers are now encouraged to share in childbirth, but our society has made a mockery of the loving, passionate participation a man can feel when he is fully involved in the drama of birth, not just a "voyeur" at delivery. The person a woman has chosen to be with her may be warmly welcomed only *as long as* he or she stays out of the way, does not question routine procedures, and goes out whenever asked to. The labor companion's main function in many births now seems to be to keep an eye on the monitoring machine so as to tell the woman in labor when her next contraction is starting. The simulated home environment of many birth rooms in hospitals offers comfort and coziness, a great improvement on the standard delivery room, but it is a caricature of the home. My five daughters were born at home, and I still cannot help being a little surprised when women, delighted with their experience in hospital birth rooms, say: ". . . and they *allowed* me to . . ."; "the doctor *encouraged* me ..."; "they *let* my husband. . . ."

This, of course, could also be said of Pithiviers. Ultimately, authority at Pithiviers, too, is in the hands of the hospital staff. But the extraordinary thing there is that Michel Odent has abrogated power to women. There is a gesture that I associate with Michel, which gives a clue to all this: he smiles, eyes shining, shrugging his shoulders, throws his hands apart, palms facing you, and asks, "Why *not*?" When women ask if they can do something, and have his approval, this is invariably his response, as it is to everything that to most other doctors would seem outrageous or mad: "Why not?"

The one thing that he will not provide is the kind of help most pregnant women expect nowadays: drugs for pain relief. When a woman books into his unit, there is an implicit contract with him not to have drugs in normal labor, but to receive everything that he can give her to help her work *with* her body rather than fighting or trying to escape from it. This is where some of us may stop and question his commitment to natural birth and the power that an obstetrician has over women in labor. If a woman is really to have a choice between alternatives, should it not extend to this, too? Is it not a basic human right to be able to have drugs for the relief of pain? Women in Sweden think so, and a law has been passed in the Swedish parliament guaranteeing complete relief of pain to all women in childbirth. The result is that a woman may start off having Demerol (to take the edge off contractions and make her drowsy), go on to an epidural (which removes all sensation from the waist down), and then, since the epidural wears off in the second stage, have a pudendal block to anesthetize the birth outlet completely.

The implications of giving this choice to women would alter the whole atmosphere of Michel Odent's unit. Midwives who now give their attention unreservedly to the woman would have to divide it between the woman and the machines. If epidurals, the most effective form of pharmacological pain relief, were introduced, there would be a strong case for introducing electronic monitoring, too. Once the body is interfered with in one way, it becomes necessary to intervene in other ways. And once feeling has been blotted out, forceps would often become necessary. There is an approximately five-times-increased risk of having a forceps delivery when a woman has had an epidural. Michel never does forceps deliveries. If women had the option of epidural anesthesia, he would be forced to. The women now actively giving birth would become patients being delivered, who have to be turned, examined, nursed before and after delivery—no longer women performing a natural function in healthy activity. This, in turn, would mean that those who did not have epidurals would inevitably receive less attention, while midwives and obstetricians busied themselves with operative delivery and "interesting cases."

There is another element in Michel Odent's thinking that is hard for some of us to accept—his insistence that birth is instinctual and something for which a woman needs no preparation but, on the contrary, must unlearn what her conscious mind has acquired. Is this another way in which women are required to adapt to a biological model of what it is to be female? A way of jettisoning reason and telling women they only need instinct in order to fulfill the maternal role?

Yet it is precisely in turning away from the consciously adopted obstetric birth in which the woman is the passive object on the delivery table, and equally from the goals of Lamaze's "painless childbirth," that we reject male views of birth in order to rediscover the essential experience for ourselves. To be "rational," to organize our most intimate experience according to the "logical" obstetric pattern of birth—or, for that matter, the athletic, goal-oriented blueprint introduced by Lamaze—is, in itself, basically to accept the male domination of birth.

Moreover, when Michel says that we must strip away the cultural excrescences of birth in order to rediscover our instinctual selves, he is not advocating any simple return to some ideal of the "primitive." In fact, he has not discarded culture. He has taken the institutional artifacts of our culture and adapted them to meet women's instinctual needs in childbirth. He works, for example, in a hospital setting, not at home, and anticipates that professionals with special skills will take part in the birth. The lights that are dimmed, the tape recorder with its music if a woman wants it during labor, the pool used for relaxation—all these are the products of industrial organization and modern civilization. But Michel uses them all to so change the hospital environment that women can give uninhibited expression to all that they feel during labor, freeing the way for *physiological* as opposed to "medicalized" birth.

Yet the impact of his work on women in Western Europe has been powerful for an insidious reason. Here is a doctor working in a hospital, part of the medical establishment, who is demonstrating that birth can be more as women want it. It is as if women are being given permission, for the first time since Dick-Read spoke out in the nineteenth century about the effect of mind and body on childbirth, to do things their way. But significantly, that permission has to be given by a physician. Something women know for themselves cannot be acknowledged, women's experiences cannot be validated, until a man, preferably a doctor in a white coat, pronounces these experiences acceptable.

Michel Odent is well aware of this paradox. He has called for the rebirth of the midwife, traditionally women's helper in labor. Indeed, he has gone further: at Pithiviers, he has recreated the art of midwifery; the midwives are the pivot on which everything else depends. It is their skill and dedication, their capacity to love, which create the special atmosphere familiar to every woman who has had a baby with midwives in attendance. They bring not only technical skills and watchfulness but warmth and joy to every birth. Those of us who have been confronted with an autocratic nurse or a doctor who has treated us like irresponsible children know that a bad relationship with those caring for you can mar even the happiest birth and turn it into a grim ordeal. The key to Michel's achievement is the good working relationship he has with the midwives, the way in which they all share a common purpose. The women who give birth at Pithiviers do not suffer from the negative consequences of bad relations between nurses and doctors, or from the ambivalent discontent of nurses who feel caught in an authoritarian obstetrical system they are powerless to control or change.

Birth, like death, is a universal experience. It may be the most powerful creative experience in many women's lives. It can either be a disruption in the flow of human existence, a fragment having little or nothing to do with the passionate longing that created the baby, or it can be lived with beauty and dignity, and labor itself can be a celebration of joy.

Birth is something that, as a woman, I share in an intense and intimate way with the Chinese peasant, the Eskimo, the woman who lives in a South American shanty town, in a nomad tent, in an African compound. This is why our way of birth is a *political* issue. It concerns every woman's right to give birth in freedom and in a loving environment. Much of what we experience as autocratic, impersonal, and degrading in women's health care generally and in the social control of our bodies is crystallized in the system of maternity care: for many of us, all over the world, cattle-market prenatal clinics and conveyor-belt obstetrics.

Birth has now become a focus for women striving for social change in male attitudes to, and treatment of, our bodies. For the first time, women in the childbirth movement—who by the very nature of their concern with home and family have in the past been apolitical—have joined hands with others to take political action. In the past, many feminists rejected the experience of birth or saw it as peripheral to their main concerns, as something that trapped women in their biological heritage. Now it is clear that this is an area in which there is an opportunity and a need for decisive action.

Changes in birthing practices that allow women to rediscover the spontaneous sexual rhythms of labor are not, by and large, coming from within obstetrics. They are coming from pressure by women to have the chance to give birth in their own way, in their own time, in an emotionally supportive setting, and with an uninhibited and joyous birth passion.

This is the challenge that Michel Odent helps us to meet—that of changing our culture of childbirth. But he is no "deliverer." He does not offer salvation to women who believe in him, although he is sometimes presented in that way. Some women actually seek out an obstetrician with this in mind, transferring onto a powerful authority figure the responsibility for their own bodies and experiences, which they are unwilling to accept. Michel would be the first to say that those who want to be guaranteed complete relief from pain or who want to hand over such responsibility should not come to him. At Pithiviers it is not the obstetrician, the hospital procedure, or the work of the team guiding the patient through labor and delivery that is at the center of the drama, but the woman herself and her intense experience. Michel loves the drama of birth, the excitement of discovering what it can be like and what women really want. He enjoys child-birth, but not as someone who directs it. Most important of all, Michel Odent *listens* to women. He is there not to dominate but to serve, not to dictate but to learn. He bears witness that every birth is a journey of exploration for all those sharing in the striving, the creative pain, the mystery, and the exultation.

—*Sheila Kitzinger*

introduction

SECOND EDITION

Why, you might ask, hasn't this second edition of *Birth Reborn* been revised and enlarged? The answer is simple. I want to highlight what was possible at a particular time in the history of childbirth (during the 1970s and early 1980s), in a particular environment—a French state hospital. *Therefore my aim is not to update the original text but to reintroduce it in the context of the 1990s.*

We have moved into another phase in the history of childbirth, and my life has taken new directions. At the time when *Birth Reborn* was first published, obstetric practices were based on beliefs and doctrines and it was still commonplace to introduce new procedures before any scientific evaluation of their implications. The prevailing belief was that it must be safer to monitor the baby's heart rate continuously during labor with an electronic machine rather than intermittently. The doctrine was that the only way to make birth safer was by introducing increasingly sophisticated electronic equipment into increasingly larger hospital units. *Birth Reborn* was challenging the dominant doctrines at the height of the electronic age.

Since that time obstetrics has become more scientific. Numerous studies have attempted to evaluate the effects of an electronic environment on the birth process, on the first contact between mother and baby, and on the beginning of breastfeeding. To do this, groups of women giving birth with electronic monitoring were compared with similar groups giving birth with intermittent auscultation. No matter what protocols were observed by the birth attendants, no matter what kind of populations were involved (high risk mothers, low risk mothers, overall, Australian, American or European), it became clear that the only constant and significant effect of an electronic environment on birth statistics is to increase the rate of intervention in general, and caesarean section in particular.

A procedure is surely dangerous when its main statistical effect is to increase the rate of intervention. A list of the studies demonstrating the dangers of electronic foetal monitoring is essential at this stage in the history of childbirth.[1-10] Not only have all the main authoritative medical journals published such studies, but their importance has been stressed by the associated comment. For example, in 1990 the *New England Journal of Medicine* published an editorial entitled 'Intrapartum Fetal Monitoring—A Disappointing Story'.[11] The conclusion was clear: 'It is unfortunate that randomised controlled trials were not carried out before this form of technology became universally applied.'

These days, any review of the authoritative medical literature leads us to the conclusion that health services should abandon electronic foetal monitoring and use the financial resources thus liberated in a different way. However, there are still doubting Thomases trying to prolong the electronic age. Some do so by replacing the visual analysis of the data by computerised analysis,[12] others by assessing the baby's electrocardiogram instead of heartbeat rhythm only,[13] and still others by using new technology such as near infrared spectroscopy. None of these attempts has been successful.

It is now clear that an electronic environment is not neutral. We have to accept that we are mammals and that all mammals have some particular strategy so as not to feel observed when giving birth. For example rats, which are active during the night, give birth during the day. To feel observed, even through the medium of a machine, alters the mother's physiological processes. *The aim now is to prepare for the post-electronic age.*

The advent of the post-electronic age might be hastened in the 1990s by a new generation of research which explores the long-term consequences of all sorts of events and interferences in the period around birth. This is absolutely new. Those who are directly involved in childbirth will have to take into account the viewpoint of researchers who were not originally concerned with childbirth.

The work of Bertil Jacobson, in Sweden, is representative of this new generation of research. He studied teenage and adult drug addiction in relation to the drugs which had been given to the subject's mother when she was in labor. The main finding was that when drugs (such as morphine, pethidine, barbiturates and laughing gas) had been administered to the mother in labor, the child was more likely to become drug addicted in later life than a contemporary whose mother had had a drug-free labor.[14]

So this second edition of *Birth Reborn* is published in a period of transition, characterised by an unprecedented discrepancy between the facts published widely in medical journals and the deep-rooted beliefs that still govern everyday attitudes. It makes its appearance at a time when I am, myself, entering a new phase of my life. As I anticipated at the end of the first edition of this book, I stopped practising as an obstetrician, that is to say, as a doctor treating the complications of pregnancy and birth. But it does not mean that I have left the field of childbirth.

I moved to London in 1985 and it was there that I began to be asked to attend births by pregnant women who could not easily find a midwife for a home birth at that time. So I became involved in the home birth movement. This has been a challenging way forward in my understanding of the effects of the environment on the birth process and the first contact between mother and baby. Even though I am still as convinced as ever that there is no future for male midwifery, my experience of thousands of normal births in this period of transition outweighs the drawbacks of my masculinity. I also take advantage of my age. I shall never be a 'grannie', but I am a grandfather.

It was also in London that I created a research unit called the Primal Health Research Centre, with the objective of exploring the correlations between the 'primal period' and what happens to us later in life.[15] The primal period encompasses life in the womb, the period around birth, and the first year after birth. One of our aims is to bring together studies from all over the world, scattered throughout various medical and scientific journals, which fall within the frame of reference of primal health research. This material is compiled into a periodic newsletter. We also conduct our own research. One study concerns a group of women who have a high intake of sea-fish in their diet. Up to now, only a very few researchers have been interested in what pregnant women eat, and anyway tended to focus on proteins and calories. In practice, the main difference between the diet of one woman and another is the balance between different families of fat. We should keep in mind that the development of the brain is a big issue where human beings are concerned, and that the foetal brain thrives on certain families of fatty acids abundant in the seafood chain.

Since I have been in London I have been able to be more flexible than when I was in charge of a maternity hospital; I can accept lecturing invitations more easily and now travel all over the world. This is another approach to evaluating how the environment influences the birth process.

It is in this context that I feel able, *in retrospect*, to make a *distinction between what was really crucial* in the big changes we introduced in Pithiviers in the 1970s and 1980s, *and what was simply the effect of a transitory fashion*, or may have been connected with purely local conditions.

* * *

Looking back now, I consider that the relative number of midwives employed in the hospital at Pithiviers, as compared with the number of obstetricians, was a matter of prime importance. Between 1977 and 1985 there were six midwives and myself attending about 1,000 births a year. When I compare different countries, different cities or different hospitals, I find that a high ratio of midwives to obstetricians is the prerequisite for good outcomes and low rates of intervention.

It is so even in the United States, a country where the rate of caesarean sections is as high as 23 per cent. In 1992 I spent three days at the Bassett General Hospital in Cooperstown, New York State. About 700 babies are born there every year. In 1988 their rate of caesarean section was 28 per cent. Then the obstetricians decided to introduce a team of 'certified nurse midwives' and gave them a great deal of autonomy. The rate of caesarean section fell to 11 per cent. The maternity service at North Central Bronx Hospital, a New York city municipal hospital for the poorer local inhabitants, has also maintained a caesarean rate of around 11 per cent, with an unselected population of disadvantaged women. In such a unit, where there are more than 3,000 deliveries a year, 85 per cent of their births are attended by a midwife. The neonatal mortality rate is 3.5 per 1,000 infants over 1,000 grammes, which is incredibly low considering the huge number of mothers 'at risk'.

An important innovation at Pithiviers, I see in retrospect, was that we provided many opportunities for women giving birth there to become familiar with the maternity hospital during pregnancy. Our singing sessions are a good example of this. The small size of the birthing room was probably another important detail. It is easier to have a feeling of privacy in a small room, especially if the light is dim. I am more aware of the importance of the size of the room since I have had the experience of home birth where, quite often, everything has been prepared for the birth of the baby in one place (for example, a mattress on the floor in the middle of a room), but eventually the baby is born elsewhere . . . and 'elsewhere' is always a small space. I am more aware now of what is wrong with the design of the birthing rooms in many hospitals or birth centres which are supposed to be 'home-like'.

In retrospect, we can also consider the use of water during labor as one of the characteristic positive changes which took place at Pithiviers. When *Birth Reborn* was first published, Pithiviers was the only hospital in the world where a birth pool was available.[16] Now there are birth pools in dozens of NHS hospitals, including several prestigious teaching establishments. Unfortunately the sensationalism of giving birth under water has sometimes obscured common sense, and the objectives about the use of birth pools have often been distorted. Some women are now prisoners of a project to give birth under water instead of listening to their bodies' needs.

Moreover, by stressing the fact that many women are attracted by water when in labor, I have contributed to the emergence of a new vision of human nature. Humans can now be seen as primates that have adapted to the land-sea interface. According to recent data in the field of genetics and molecular biology, many similarities have been found between *Homo sapiens* and the chimpanzees. The genetic distance between us and the chimpanzees is smaller than the gap between gorilla and chimpanzee, or between two species of gibbon. And the more the gap between man and the chimpanzees closes, the features that make humans distinct become more and more intriguing. All of them, taken one by one, can be interpreted

as adaptation to the sea.[17] For example, our large brain, four times bigger than the brain of the chimpanzees. We know now that the fatty acids which are essential for feeding the brain are abundant only in the seafood chain. It is not by chance that sea mammals have larger brains than their cousins on the land. The fact that we express our emotions by shedding salty tears, the general shape of our body which facilitates bepedalism, our sexual behaviour, our low larynx, are among the other features which can be interpreted as adaptation to the sea. This new version of *Homo sapiens* tends to suggest that the use of water during labor is not a fad or a fashion.[18]

From a practical point of view, the use of water during labor can be understood as a substitute for drugs. At Pithiviers, we reached a stage where the use of drugs was almost completely eliminated. This fact has to be stressed today more than it might have been in the past, because more and more studies suggest the long-term negative effects of drugs used in obstetrics. And we must consider not only the side effects of drugs used during labor and delivery, but also all the drugs used during pregnancy and the whole period surrounding birth. For example, we know now that the so-called 'tocolytic' drugs, which inhibit the contraction of the uterus during pregnancy, do not in fact reduce the risks of premature birth, and their side effects are well documented. So my negative comments about these drugs, which were provocative in the first edition, are unlikely to incite much comment any more. In the first edition, I omitted to mention that newborn babies at Pithiviers were not injected with vitamin K, as is done routinely in many hospitals to prevent an exceptionally rare disease—haemorrhagic disease of the newborn—which is related to vitamin K deficiency. Our argument then was that no study had ever tried to evaluate the possible long-term effects of such injections. It is only now, in the 1990s, that British, Scandinavian and American studies are tackling these issues. It is too soon to draw final conclusion.[19, 20, 21]

Not only do modern babies receive drugs, but they are also exposed to ultrasound scans. My comments in the first edition of *Birth Reborn*, that 'for the most part, ultrasound findings, however interesting, are useless for all practical purposes', were considered too provocative to be really serious. But those comments do not differ greatly from the point of view expressed in an editorial in the *New England Journal of Medicine* ten years later, in 1993.[22] This editorial was inspired by a huge multi-centre study[23] which found there is no medical reason to propose a routine ultrasound scan to 80 per cent of the population of pregnant women. At the same time, hard data were published suggesting that exposure to ultrasound in the womb might have long-term effects. According to Norwegian statistics involving more than 2,000 eight- or nine-year olds, there is a correlation between routine ultrasound scans and being left-handed.[24] This is enough to suggest that ultrasound does have some effect on the development of the brain. According to an Australian study, frequently exposure to ultrasound might impair foetal growth.[25]

To claim that forceps were an obsolete tool was also a provocative statement in the early 1980s. In our practice, when there was a need for mechanical intervention at a birth, it was either some gentle assistance with a vacuum extractor by the vaginal route, or a caesarean section. Now many studies have demonstrated the advantages of the vacuum extractor as against the use of forceps, especially where damage to the maternal tissues is concerned.

While many aspects of our attitudes and innovations at Pithiviers can be looked back upon as avant-grade, positive, and based on fundamental needs, some of the changes we introduced were, rather, the effects of a transitory fashion. A case in point was the requirement that a bath should be given to the baby in the hour following birth, which was obviously influenced by the popular book by Frederic Leboyer, published in 1974.[26] In fact, after a birth in a warm, small space, in complete privacy, the mother who does not feel guided and observed wants to keep her baby in her arms and is not anxious to give him or her a bath immediately.

These transitory fashions are not really dangerous. But there are some aspects of *Birth Reborn* that I see now as potentially harmful. There are many photos in the book, which may cultivate the idea that it is harmless to bring a camera into a birthing place, whereas the priority should be to eliminate all onlookers, and all their different ways of observing.

We were faced with a dilemma which must be explained. In the early 1980s it was imperative to do away with many of the old mental images associated with words like 'delivery' and 'birth', and to put forward pictures that showed alternatives to childbirth with the mother on a table, under bright lights, surrounded by guides and coaches. We were always anxious to introduce the camera only at the very last moment, just before the birth, at the point of no return, when there was no risk of stopping the progress of delivery. Now the priority is much more to halt the epidemic of photos and videos. In my last book, *The Nature of Birth and Breastfeeding*, there are no pictures at all.[27]

Another possible danger with an illustrated book is to look at the pictures without reading the text. In the case of *Birth Reborn* there is a danger that one might get the impression that it is the position of the woman in labor which is important. Her position is the consequence of her hormonal balance, and so is influenced by the degree of her sense of privacy. Let us consider, for example, the time when the baby is about to be born: When the mother has a sudden tendency to be upright and to grasp something or somebody, it means that she is releasing a great

amount of hormones of the adrenaline family. It is not the upright posture which is significant; it is her need to be upright.[28]

When looking at the pictures without reading the text, there is also the risk that one might consider the participation of the baby's father an undisputed necessity. In fact it is worth remembering that this behaviour— new in the history of humanity, and even in the history of the mammals—started as an adaptation to absolutely new situations: births happening in large hospitals, the predominantly nuclear family, and the disappearance of the autonomous midwife. Because the participation of the father at a birth is a new phenomenon we shall probably need several decades before being able to evaluate all its implications. We must not only consider how the man can influence the physiological processes, but also how his participation in the birth can influence the future of sexual attraction between the couple. We have to be careful before introducing new doctrines.

We must also take care over the words we use, and their conditioning power. If I had revised the first edition I would have deleted any word suggesting that a woman does not have the power to give birth by herself. There would be no chapter called 'Helping Women in Labor'. Nobody can help an involuntary process. The point is not to disturb it. Western women are really conditioned to feel that they cannot give birth without being dependent on somebody else. In medical books terms such as 'labor management' and 'patients' are too common. In books about 'natural childbirth', terms such as 'coaching', 'guiding', 'support' have the same conditioning effect.

In a revised edition of *Birth Reborn* I would make more frequent use of the key word 'privacy'. This word has no equivalent in French, and the original text was a translation from the French. To give due importance to the word 'privacy' tends to reverse current western conditioning and to introduce a cascade of new concepts. To have a feeling of privacy you must feel secure. To feel secure, you must feel protected. To feel protected is probably a basic need for the woman in labor and for the mother welcoming her baby. Let us recall that the first midwives were substitutes for the mother of the woman in labor, and a mother is, first and foremost, a protective person. These days we must analyse our cultural conditioning and rediscover the roots of midwifery.

If preceded by such warnings, a book *which was provocative in the early 1980s might become a useful tool at the dawn of the post-electronic age*. Changing hospitals and designing really home-like birth centres are indeed the two main strategies for embarking on this new age, although there is a third possible way. It would be to follow the Dutch model and to adapt home birth to our modern urbanised society. But this cannot be done overnight. The old, long-held beliefs are still stronger than the facts, and many responsible professionals have not yet developed their scientific minds to a point where they are ready to draw objective conclusions from the wonderful birth statistics in the Netherlands.[29]

That is why, while it is 'time to think again,'[30] we should now reconsider what could be learnt from a maternity unit which had entered the post-electronic age as early as the 1970s.

Michel Odent
London
October 1993

1 Haverkamp, A.D. et al. The evaluation of continuous fetal heart monitoring in high risk pregnancy. *Am. J. Obstet. Gynecol.* 1976; 125: 310-20.

2 Haverkamp, A.D., *et al*. A controlled trial of the differential effects of intrapartum monitoring. *Am. J. Obstet. Gynecol.* 1979; 134: 399-412.

3 Renou, P., Chang, A., Anderson, I., Wood, C. Controlled trial of fetal intensive care. *Am. J. Obstet. Gynecol.* 1976; 126: 470-76.

4 Wood, C. A comparison of two controlled trials concerning the efficacy of fetal intensive care. *J. Perinat. Med.* 1978; 6: 140-53.

5 Kelso, I. M. *et al*. An assessment of continuous fetal heart rate monitoring in labor *Am. J. Obstet. Gynecol.* 1978; 131: 526-32.

6 Wood, C. *et al*. A controlled trial of fetal heart rate monitoring in low-risk obstetric population. *Am. J. Obstet. Gynecol.* 1981; 141; 527-34.

7 MacDonald, D., Chalmers, I. *et al*. The Dublin randomised controlled trial of intrapartum fetal heart rate monitoring. *Am. J. Obstet. Gynecol.* 1985; 152: 524-39.

8 Leveno, K. J. *et al*. A prospective comparison of selective and universal electronic fetal monitoring in 34, 995 pregnancies. *N. Engl. J. Med.* 1986; 315: 615-19.

9 Prentice, A., Lind, T. Fetal heart rate monitoring during labour—too frequent intervention, too little benefit. *Lancet*. 1987; 2:1375-1377.

10 Shy, K. K., Luthy, D. A., Bennett, F. C. *et al*. Effects of electronic monitoring, as compared with periodic auscultation, on the neurological development of premature infants. *N. Engl. J. Med*. 1990; 322: 588-93.

11 Freeman, R. Intrapartum fetal monitoring—A disappointing story. *N. Engl. J. Med*. 1990; 322: 624-6.

12 Pello, L. C. *et al*. Computerised fetal heart analysis in labor. *Am. J. Obstet. Gynecol*. 1991; 78: 602-10.

13 Westgate, J. *et al*. Randomised trial of cardiotocography alone or with ST waveform analysis for intrapartum monitoring. *Lancet*. 1992; pp.194-198.

14 Jacobson, B., Nyberg, K. *et al*. Opiate addiction in adult offspring through possible imprinting after obstetric treatment. *British Medical Journal*. 1990; 301: 1067-70.

15 Odent, M. *Primal Health*. Century-Hutchinson. London, 1986.

16 Odent, M. Birth under water. *Lancet*. Dec. 24 1983. pp.1476-77

17 Morgan, E. *The Aquatic Ape*. Souvenir Press, 1982.

18 Odent, M. *Water and Sexuality*. Penguin. London, 1990.

19 Golding, I. *et al*. Childhood cancer, intramuscular vitamin K, and pethidine given during labour. *British Medical Journal*. 1992; 305: 341-6.

20 Ekelund, H. *et al*. Administration of vitamin K to newborn infants and childhood cancer. *British Medical Journal*. 1993; 307: 89-91.

21 Kiebanoff, M. A., Read, J. S. *et al*. The risk of childhood cancer after neonatal exposure to vitamin K. *N. Engl. J. Med*. 1993; 329: 905-8.

22 Berkowitz, R. Should every pregnant woman undergo ultrasonography? Editorial. *N. Engl. J. Med*. 1993; 329:874-5.

23 Ewigman, B. *et al*. Effect of prenatal ultrasound screening on perinatal outcome. *N. Engl. J. Med*. 1993; 329:821-7.

24 Salvesen, K. A. *et al*. Routine ultrasonography in utero and subsequent handedness and neurological development. *British Medical Journal*. 1993; 307:159-64.

25 Newnham, J. P. *et al*. Effects of frequent ultrasound during pregnancy: A randomised controlled trial. *Lancet*. 1993; 342: 887-91.

26 Leboyer, F. *Pour une naissance safis violence*. Le Seuil. Paris, 1974.

27 Odent, M. *The Nature of Birth and Breastfeeding*. Bergin and Garvey (Greenwood). New York, 1992.

28 Odent, M. Position in delivery. *Lancet*. May 12 1990 (letter) p.1166.

29 Odent, M. *Planned home birth in industrialised countries*. WHO report. Copenhagen, 1991.

30 Keirse, M. Frequent prenatal ultrasound: Time to think again. *Lancet*. 1993; 342: 878-9.

birth reborn

Pithiviers

pithiviers

I first came to Pithiviers in 1962 to take charge of general surgery at the public hospital. The results of a placement examination brought me by chance to this town of ten thousand, which I soon grew quite fond of. Only a short distance from Paris, the region around Pithiviers still offers all the advantages of country living. The land is fertile, planted with wheat and sugar beets. The local farmers still keep bees, hunt larks, and gather together with their neighbors every Saturday at the village market. Though mainly agricultural, the area is sprinkled with small trades and factories, including a biscuit company and a sugar refinery. All in all, Pithiviers is the kind of place rarely shown to tourists. It is just another anonymous small town like so many others. In fact, most French people associate Pithiviers only with a popular cake made in and named for the town; they have no idea where Pithiviers is.

When I started my work here, I learned that I was also expected to oversee a small maternity clinic in the hospital. The clinic

Entering Pithiviers hospital

My previous experience in obstetrics was minimal and scattered over the course of many years. During the early fifties, I had spent six months as an intern in a large maternity ward in Paris. In those days it was common for five or six women in labor to occupy one large room. Birth took place in a factory-like atmosphere where fear was contagious. Doctors often used forceps, and rarely performed cesareans. I remember the chief obstetrician only because a famous style of forceps (the Suzor forceps) was named after him. I took very little interest in the internship, and had no idea that I would ever practice obstetrics.

Later, during my military service as a war surgeon in the Berber region of Algeria, I was occasionally called in when obstetrical care was necessary. From time to time, pregnant women would come down from the mountains at the very last moment to give birth, and I would be asked to do a cesarean or forceps delivery, or to attend to uterine ruptures. Soon afterward, stationed in Guinea, I was witness to the constant struggle between African women who wanted to stand or squat during labor and European doctors and midwives who insisted that they give birth lying down. I sided with the doctors at the time, and didn't give these isolated episodes much thought.

When I came to Pithiviers, I naturally relied a great deal on the midwives' guidance. Gisèle, who had been at the clinic for some time, was very experienced. Gabrielle, who

was frequented mainly by women from Pithiviers and the nearby villages, but they came from extremely diverse backgrounds. Some were factory workers, farmers, merchants, or civil servants. Some were immigrants from Portugal, North Africa, or even the Far East. The clinic accepted everyone who came: there was no "screening," from either a social or a medical point of view.

At that time there was only one midwife at the clinic, and she was totally responsible for its day-to-day operation. She would call me in only when a doctor was needed to perform a cesarean or a forceps delivery. Since, as a surgeon, I had been trained to do things like remove gall bladders and repair broken limbs, these procedures seemed simply a natural extension of my technical skills. As for obstetrics, I had only the sketchiest notions about its practice.

joined us soon after my arrival, was young, energetic, just out of school, and very enthusiastic about psychoprophylaxis, the "Lamaze method."* It wasn't so much what they actually said or did that made me really pay attention to obstetrics for the first time, but rather the fact that the fifteen-to-twenty-year interval between the times they had each studied midwifery had made such a difference in their respective practices. For instance, Gisèle, who was older, would wait patiently for the baby to be born. At the end of the delivery, she would simply say: "Don't hold back, relax, let yourself go. . . ." Gabrielle, on the other hand, was eager to prepare a woman from the start of pregnancy, to help her with breathing during labor, and to encourage her to control herself during birth. In the final stages of labor, Gabrielle would give precise commands, such as: "Breathe in, breathe out . . . control your breathing . . . push. . . ." Their differences shed a new light on obstetrical practice for me; I began to realize that it consisted of more than mechanics and techniques. And I saw more and more how much a woman's experience of labor depended on the personality and attitude of the attendant. Women were attracted by Gabrielle's youthful enthusiasm and expressed a greater interest in her, but they were probably more likely to have an easy birth with Gisèle.

Although I officially remained a surgeon, as time went on I became increasingly involved in life at the maternity unit. I found that the principles on which I based my surgical work—simplification and the elimination of useless procedures—could be applied to obstetrics as well. My past experiences as a practitioner had already led me to believe that time and patience are the most useful of allies, and that active intervention should be used only sparingly and in special cases. With obstetrics as with general surgery, I was convinced that keeping intrusive interference to a minimum creates fewer immediate risks, while at the same time producing better long-term results. And paradoxically, my lack of actual training in obstetrics left me more open to learning through experience. I found myself questioning the most accepted procedures. "Why do you break the waters?" I would ask the midwives. "Why do you cut the umbilical cord so soon after birth?" Often they would answer: "Because this is what we were taught in school."

But as we explored the reasons why we did certain things, little by little a scarcely noticeable change took place. We became less dogmatic and began to experiment. One day a

*The "Lamaze method," or "psychoprophylaxis," is a way of preparing for childbirth developed in the 1950s by Fernand Lamaze, a French doctor. Lamaze trained women to respond to labor contractions with different types of breathing, which quicken as the contractions become more intense. This concentration on breathing is supposed to take a woman's attention away from the pain of labor. Over recent years "Lamaze" teachers have become more eclectic in their approach to labor but traditional "Lamaze" is still common in many parts of the United States and Europe.

midwife gave an infant a bath to calm him, even though he was only two days old. From that day on, we no longer accepted the French and American "rule" that forbids regular bathing of babies until the umbilical cord has fallen off. Another time, a baby found its mother's breast moments after birth and, to everyone's astonishment, began to nurse in the delivery room. I wondered why such an apparently gratifying event occurred so rarely. The answer, of course, was simple: it is common hospital practice to separate mother and child from the moment of birth, in order to weigh or measure the infant and give it a general physical check-up. Again and again, such new experiences led us to question conventional obstetrics. We did not know where we were going, but we were on our way.

Gradually, as our practice changed, so did our attitude. Before coming to Pithiviers, I had known little of the world but doctors and patients. I had looked at people from a narrow medical perspective; I had shared the conventional view of childbirth as a "medical problem" requiring technical "solutions." I had grown used to hearing doctors speak of pregnant women as "patients." Not long ago I lectured at a German university, and an obstetrician provided a simultaneous translation. Whenever I used the phrase "pregnant woman" or "woman in labor," he would translate these as "patient" and could not understand why the students objected so ve-

hemently. Obviously, this attitude is not confined to obstetrics. Often medical articles refer to "methods" and "material"—"material" meaning people. In all medical fields, such a mentality contributes to an increased reliance on drugs, electronic monitoring, and surgical intervention. At Pithiviers, as I came to know my "patients" as individuals and not simply as medical case histories, I had to revise my perspective.

Even though I was a surgeon, women would often come to me to talk about a variety of subjects, from marriage to birth control. In the family-planning groups I joined to inform myself, discussions moved beyond a medical frame of reference, beyond issues of contraception and birth to sexuality, personal feelings, and social expectations. People talked about why they did or didn't want to have children; related their private experiences of labor, delivery, and breastfeeding; and spoke of the subtle connections between fertility and self-image for men and women. I became convinced that birth, far from being a "medical problem," was in fact an integral part of sexual and emotional life.

Certainly at our clinic I witnessed this truth daily. For both men and women, childbirth was an intense, intimate, all-encompassing experience. As the doctor, I was far from the central figure in the drama; at times I even felt like an intruder. Even as the prevalent view of childbirth as a medical event transformed maternity units throughout the world into high-tech laboratories and human

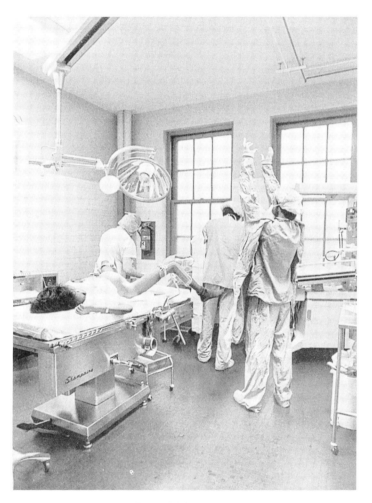

Typical delivery room

beings into passive objects, our recognition of birth as an emotional and sexual experience led us at Pithiviers to see ourselves, on the contrary, as simply facilitators, a kind of medical back-up team whose task was to intervene as *little* as possible.

Since so much of what we were doing was new to us, we naturally sought to place it in some kind of intellectual context. Two new young midwives, Dominique and Marie-José, arrived at the clinic in 1969 and fell in easily with this spirit of exploration. Certified for just a short time, they knew obstetrics only as it was practiced in the teaching hospitals, but were adventurous and ready to reconsider what they had learned. We all eagerly read Ivan Illich's *Medical Nemesis* and extended his observation that doctors are often the slaves, not the masters, of the technology they apply to the practice of obstetrics in industrialized societies. Reading Frederic Leboyer's *Birth Without Violence,* we felt immediate sympathy with his concern for the infant's experience of birth.

Leboyer created a language new to most doctors—a language that spoke to our sensitivity and emotions as well as to our intellect. He showed us the newborn not as an object unable to see, hear, or feel, but rather as a human creature in need of warmth and nurture. In short, Leboyer was the first doctor to express what many women intuitively know about their babies in spite of the medical establishment's advice to the contrary. Leboyer gave us at Pithiviers a frame in which to understand our actions and put them into practice. Under his influence, our birthing room became a quieter and more peaceful place, more welcoming to the infant. We encouraged prolonged contact between mother and child. Mothers were free to nurse their babies right after birth and to bathe them if they wanted to. The alertness we observed in both mother and child confirmed us in our decision not to use drugs or intervene unnecessarily.

As for myself, life seemed to be pulling me in two different directions. On the one hand, I was spending more and more time in the maternity unit. On the other, there was my surgical practice, which still intrigued me, posing divergent yet related problems. My method of treating fractures differed from conventional procedures in much the same way that childbirth at Pithiviers differs from conventional obstetrics. But seriously to call into question the foundations of both modern traumatology and obstetrics at the same time was beyond me. I had to make a choice. In 1972, a colleague of mine took over direction of both traumatology and orthopedics, diminishing to that extent my continuing responsibilities as head of the surgical unit. I was finally able to devote myself more fully to obstetrics.

The atmosphere at Pithiviers during this

time was one of great excitement. We experimented even more often now, trying out new practices, giving up on others. One day, for example, during a birth, we let the baby's head come out all by itself, without our touching or supporting it or the mother's perineum. Another day, we decided that the rubber gloves we wore were unnecessary. Every new step we took affected each of us differently. For Dominique, it was very difficult to stop wearing gloves, while Marie-José had a harder time giving up the common practice of speeding up labor by breaking the bag of waters that surrounds the unborn baby.

A psychologist who had just given birth at the clinic started Friday-night groups where future parents could come to hear about the work we were doing. These meetings soon included not only women and couples from the immediate area, but also interested people from far-off places who had specific reasons for seeking us out. A number of people inspired by Leboyer, for example, came to Pithiviers so that they could bring their children into the world as they wished, gently. Others came simply to talk, to share their feelings of hope, fear, disappointment, enthusiasm, excitement.

Such an atmosphere certainly made for greater expressive freedom during labor and birth. However, there were still limits. Our birth setting remained what it had always been: a conventional delivery room with ob-

Michel Odent and midwife Marie-José Matheault

stetrical table, bright lights, and a multitude of surgical paraphernalia. The mood was oppressively medical and impersonal, clearly incompatible with our transformed view of childbirth as an intimate, even sexual, experience. Moreover, we could see that the delivery table, the most prominent piece of furniture in the room, seriously infringed on the mother-to-be's freedom of action. By its mere presence, it suggested a reclining position and gave a woman little choice but to lie down and labor on her back. This traditional dorsal position is in fact the worst possible alternative physiologically for both mother and child: when a woman lies on her back,

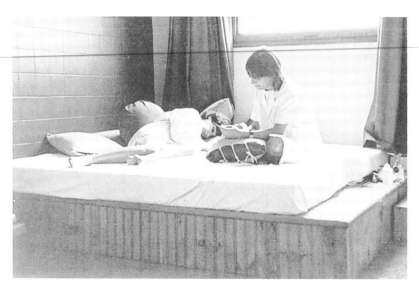

Woman in labor and midwife Dominique Pourré
in the "salle sauvage"

the enlarged uterus compresses the major blood vessels, which in turn diminishes the amount of oxygenated blood entering and leaving the placenta. In addition, such a position makes it impossible for a woman to take advantage of gravity to facilitate delivery.

To encourage women to try other birth positions, we replaced our old delivery room with a new one designed by women who had themselves given birth at Pithiviers. Our *"salle sauvage"* (or primitive room), as we call it, is built for privacy, comfort, and freedom of motion. Painted in warm, cheerful colors, and furnished with a firm, low platform and bright-colored cushions, (but with no bed or table that would impose one particular labor

position), it is intimate, homelike, and welcoming—very much in keeping with our belief that a place to give birth should be more like a place to make love than a hospital room. This birthing room, however, represented more than just attractive decor or a strategy to encourage a variety of labor positions: it was a place where a woman could do exactly as she liked, feel physically and emotionally free to act and move about as she wished. It was our first concrete step toward giving childbirth back to women.

To do so, to give birth back to women, is no small ambition. The history of obstetrics, after all, is largely the history of the gradual exclusion of mothers from their central role in the birth process. Modern obstetrics origi-

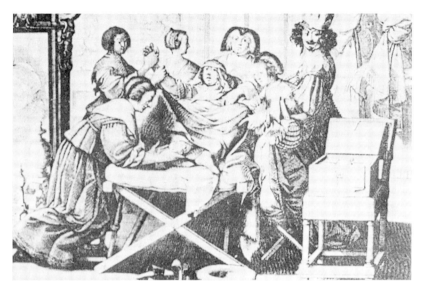

Belgium, seventeenth century. A new figure enters the traditional birthing scene: the male physician with his box containing metal forceps.

nated in seventeenth-century France when male doctors first entered the birthing room and assumed the traditional role of midwives. For the first time women were required to give birth lying on their backs, so that doctors could use their forceps more easily. Tradition has it that this practice began when Louis XIV had his mistress endure labor in this position so that he could have a better view of the birth of his child from his hiding place behind a curtain. Since that time, the obstetrician—instruments in hand, in control—has always stood before a passive, supine woman. (Indeed, the very word "obstetric" is derived from the Latin *ob* + *stare*, which means "to stand before.") The dorsal position and the enforced passivity

that it imposes on the mother have today become all but universal in industrial societies. So has the replacement of midwives by doctors, which indicates a profound devaluation of the maternal sensitivity and care midwives as women can bring to other women.

A whole range of standard obstetrical practices reflects a similar downgrading of the woman's role in childbirth. For example, the alacrity with which doctors today prescribe bedrest, sew up the cervix, and paralyze the uterus with drugs to prevent prematurity; the separation of mother and newborn; the automatic advice that women stay in bed after birth; and the readiness with which doctors counsel mothers to stop breastfeeding— all depreciate the mother's central role.

Conventional psychoprophylaxis—the La- maze method—does the same thing in a more subtle way. Here the woman actually colludes in her own denial, by adopting a system that "controls" her response to pain, her breathing, her position, and even the sounds she makes—the most basic aspects of a laboring woman's behavior. And although Leboyer's insights into the child's experience of birth gave rise to a new consciousness in our clinic and in the world at large, childbirth professionals have regrettably managed to interpret his idea of "birth without violence" as the "Leboyer method," in which attention is focused on the child to the exclusion of the mother. Sadly, the same phenomena exist in the East as in the West. When I visited China recently, I was disappointed to find that, al- though the majority of obstetricians are women, they do their best to copy Occidental practices, and make the same mistakes.

Our "salle sauvage" was part of our effort to counter the tide that had swept women aside and left them with only a marginal role in childbirth, and to restore them to their proper, central place. Our experience repeat- edly confirmed the rightness of our ap- proach, by demonstrating the skill and knowledge of the woman in charge of bring- ing her child into the world.

We had often observed—without under- standing the cause—that women seemed to forget themselves and what was going on around them during the course of an unmed- icated labor. For instance, one day we hap- pened to film a birth with a large TV camera. Several minutes after the baby was born, the young mother said: "It's too bad that no one was around to photograph the birth." Many women in labor undergo similar changes in their level of consciousness. They get a faraway look in their eyes, forget social con- ventions, lose self-consciousness and self- control. Many let out a characteristic cry at the moment of delivery. We noted, however, that women in this state are far from being helpless, lost, or without "expertise." In- stead, they act deliberately, spontaneously seeking and easily finding the positions that

The moment of birth . . .

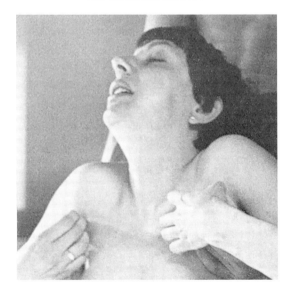

suit them best, and that also turn out to be the most efficient physiologically. Without being told, they know how to hold and nurture their babies immediately after birth, just as a newborn knows how to seek out its mother's breast. This seems true for women of all cultural backgrounds at our clinic. After seeing how much tribal births filmed in New Guinea and South Africa resembled births in our own *"salle sauvage,"* I became even more convinced that there was some universal component in the behavior of mother and newborn, and that—given the right kind of environment, where she could feel free and uninhibited—a woman could naturally reach a level of response deeper within her than individuality, upbringing, or culture.

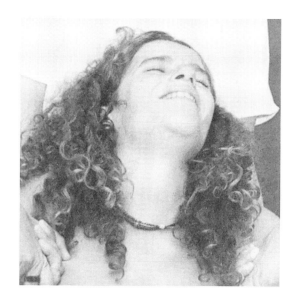

I have found it very difficult to describe this shift to a deeper level of consciousness during labor. I had thought of calling it "regression," but I know that the word sounds pejorative, evoking a return to some animal state. "Instinct" is a better term, although it, too, resonates with moralistic overtones. Women are frequently told that they should "instinctively" do or feel certain things and that they are lacking if they don't. Furthermore, the word "instinct" is often unfavorably contrasted with reason—women are said to be "instinctive," men "rational" —as if one could not be instinctive and rational at the same time. But there is nothing shameful or sexist in recognizing that instinct plays a part in our behaviors, especially those that exist at the intersection of nature and culture, such as lovemaking, labor, or the newborn's search for the mother's nipple. People can and do benefit enormously from rediscovering and exploiting to the fullest their instinctive potential on these occasions. As women in labor move and act according to their instincts, they are in fact behaving extremely rationally, and thus generally have faster and easier deliveries than women who do not. At Pithiviers, therefore, we strive to create a climate in which women can, in this sense, "forget" themselves.

It now seems evident that the instinctive state that enables a woman to labor sponta-

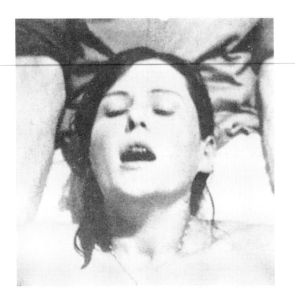

cold or afraid, a calm, reassuring environment in which a woman can relax is always beneficial. It has also become more and more obvious that endorphins play an important role in the complex hormonal equilibrium that makes a spontaneous delivery possible. Neurohormones with morphinelike functions, these "endogenous opiates," act as natural painkillers, not only protecting against pain but also suppressing anxiety and inducing a general feeling of well-being. High levels of endorphins may, for example, induce the so-called alpha brain waves that are associated with states of serenity or beatitude. It's almost as if people have always sensed the presence of this natural capacity for well-being and sought ways to trigger it. Running, for example, raises our endorphin levels; prayer, meditation, yoga, and acupuncture may do the same.

The discovery of the body's endogenous opiates explained something that had puzzled me long ago. While performing surgery during the war, I was surprised on several occasions to find unmedicated soldiers with severe injuries acting as if they had taken painkillers—or as if their bodies had secreted some special substance to protect them from suffering. In just the same way, women during labor often act as if they are "naturally" drugged and remark on how well they feel between painful contractions. I have even seen women labor in virtually ecstatic states. But in order for the body's natural powers to

neously is connected with a particular hormonal balance. The exact nature of this balance is not yet known. We do know that the posterior pituitary gland has to secrete the hormone oxytocin in order for uterine contractions to begin and to continue.* On the other hand, we know that the secretion of adrenaline-like substances can inhibit labor contractions or intensify their pain, as it can inhibit nursing and intense moments of sexuality. Since these adrenaline-like substances are typically secreted when one is

*Some recent studies suggest that oxytocin can make people forgetful. It may thus play a role in defending against pain.

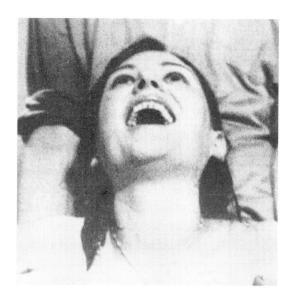

forces all aspects of sexual and reproductive behavior. Scientists are discovering connections between endorphins and oxytocin—the hormone that, among its other functions, stimulates uterine contractions during orgasm, labor, and delivery—and between endorphins and prolactin—the hormone that stimulates milk secretion. Breastfeeding, in turn, seems to raise the endorphin level. And since endorphins are known to foster attachment and also to contribute to "grooming" (that is, caregiving, affectionate) behaviors, their presence in high levels in both mother and child immediately following spontaneous delivery suggests that there may well be a hormonal basis for the process of attachment that occurs in the first hours and days after birth.[1] Overall, the existence of these complex neurohormones confirms our belief in the interconnection of all aspects of sexual life, and—since the balanced secretion of hormones is a delicate matter, highly responsive to external conditions and psychological states—presents another powerful argument against medical interference in, or disturbance of, the physiology of the labor process.

come into play, they must be left alone. To give women painkilling drugs and synthetic hormones (artificial oxytocin) during birth, as is common practice in most modern hospitals, will destroy the hormonal balance on which spontaneous labor depends. Certainly pain itself can slow labor down, but when drugs are not used, the body can defend itself effectively and naturally against it. Indeed, it has been found that the longer and more difficult a woman's labor, the higher her endorphin level will be.

This endorphin system not only plays a crucial role in labor, but also functions as a type of intrinsic "reward system" that rein-

With our decision to let *women* give birth to their children, to leave women free to labor as they wished, Pithiviers definitively assumed its particular character. Wherever we looked, labor and birth were becoming more "medicalized," more technological, while at our clinic these events were simply the affairs of mother and child. Everywhere around us, we saw doctors increasing their use of drugs and artificial intervention, while at Pithiviers we kept intervention to an absolute minimum, and considered drugs unnecessary and harmful. Today obstetrics still focuses on the role of the doctor and his preoccupation with how best to control and master childbirth. Especially in the United States, this attitude has resulted in the systematic concentration of normal births in environments equipped with advanced technology and routine electronic surveillance.* Modern obstetrics knows nothing and cares less about the fact that labor, birth, and early nursing are integral parts of a woman's sexual life. As a medical discipline, it remains unaware of the potentially negative impact of male doctors and strangers on the unfolding of labor, and equally ignorant of the importance of female birth attendants and midwives. Over the years, our practice at Pithiviers has called the very basis of modern obstetrics into question to such an extent that the very word "obstetrics" now seems foreign and outdated to us.

Our clinic has grown. There are now seven midwives. The number of births here has quintupled over the last twenty years. Like all obstetricians, we at Pithiviers are haunted by the ever-present specter of risk. But our experiences have clearly shown that an approach which "demedicalizes" birth, restores dignity and humanity to the process of childbirth, and returns control to the mother is also the safest approach. Our policy works by any standard, for we have noted a marked decrease in risk for both mother and infant; indeed, our results compare favorably with the best in the world. At a time when most industrialized countries cannot keep perinatal* mortality rates below 10/1000 without simultaneously increasing the rate of interventions and cesareans (which is often as high as 20 percent), at Pithiviers, with *no screening whatsoever*, we attain the same low mortality rates with a cesarean rate of only 6–7 percent. This is the most dramatic evidence that our approach, which transforms the experience of childbirth, is a safe and sound alternative.

For all who ask themselves the same questions we do—for women who wish to reclaim childbirth, for parents who want to experience birth as an intimate event, for clinicians who welcome a radical rethinking of their practice—here is how childbirth happens at Pithiviers.

*Hospitals in Great Britain, largely in response to the organized efforts of concerned women, have a better record of resisting or turning back this trend, though much progress remains to be made.

Perinatal refers to babies after six months' gestation and before the age of seven days. The perinatal mortality rate in the United States is 18/1000; the cesarean rate 19 percent.

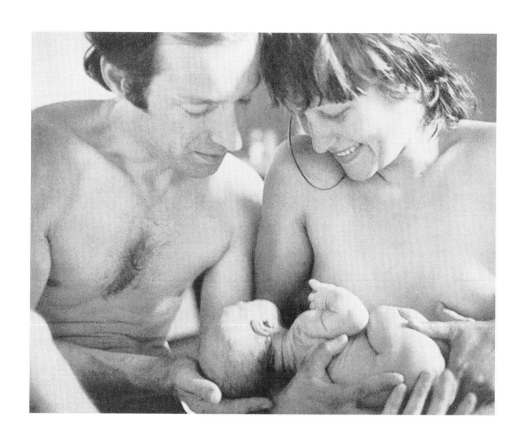

After two normal births during which I had, none-theless, suffered all the standard interventions of conventional obstetrics, I was determined that my third delivery would be different. If all went well, I was prepared to find a midwife and insist on a home birth. But an ultrasound scan confirmed that the baby was breech at thirty-four weeks, and no one was confident that it would turn. The doctor at the local hospital suggested that a date be decided upon for me to be induced and said that an epidural and forceps would be used. If that didn't work, I understood that cesareans were quite common for breech babies.

The old depression returned. I had desperately wanted this baby's birth to be natural, and there was no choice of hospital other than the same one that had all the associations of the last confine-ment, when I had felt that the baby had been taken from me. On that occasion, as I was stitched, I asked the doctor, "Why are we less efficient in childbirth than animals?" I already felt that the birth had been ruined for me, and I was troubled by the amount of "routine" intervention in what I had considered to be a normal physiological event. His response was, "It's an entirely different matter for animals." He implied that women are not efficient in childbirth. I had seen this doctor at prenatal visits and he seemed to have understood my wishes for the birth. Despite this, he had man-aged my labor for his own convenience, and my nervous system felt shattered for months after-ward. I had postpartum depression that I knew was not simply hormonal in origin. I felt cheated almost to the point of grieving. Yet now my hopes for a better experience seemed doomed. This was to be, to my mind, another "factory" baby.

I had heard about Pithiviers; I knew that women traveled there from other countries. However, I could hardly envisage it as a real possibility for me —I was by now thirty-seven weeks pregnant. Still, I rang Dr. Odent a few days later, when I had decided that I would regret it forever if I did not gather my strength and make an effort to go to Pithiviers. I asked if I could come. He said, "Why not?" When I said that the baby was breech, he replied, "It makes no difference." I immediately felt confident and energetic about the proposed journey.

My husband and I knew very well that time would be short if an emergency arose. Set against this risk was the inevitable recurrence of my depression; before we made the decision to go to Pithiviers, it had already started again. I knew *that I could not relive the depression that I experienced after my last confinement and expect to function as a wife and mother to three young children. At my last prenatal check in England, I was nearly in despair as the nurse explained, with the aid of a doll, how breech babies are delivered. I heard myself protesting as never before in my three pregnancies. I said to my doctor, "If you send me to that hospital again, that will finish me." The nurse made me feel ashamed, exclaiming, "If that baby could hear you talking!" I suddenly realized that I really had rejected "the system" for the first time in my life. I no longer cared who thought I was making a fuss. I had previously been so polite and helpful to all the medical personnel, and it had*

got me nowhere—even my own children had been born for me, and this was probably my last chance to take what life has to offer. I just had to take responsibility for myself for a change, and Pithiviers offered an alternative that attracted me. Even its distance from home appealed to me. I felt a certain animal longing to get away from it all, to have privacy from the people I knew and to find a special place to give birth. I had to get to Pithiviers before labor began. This baby was going to be mine and safely mine. I said to my doctor, "Things are changing, though, aren't they?" "Yes," he replied, " but that is in a foreign country." My husband informed him later that that was exactly where we were going.

Welcome to Pithiviers

before

Every pregnant woman comes to us with a unique personal, family, and cultural history that will strongly influence the course of her labor. In some cultures, labor seems easier as a rule than in others. In some families, too, there is virtually a tradition of easy birth. A woman brings to childbirth her entire life experience, reaching as far back as her own infancy and birth. We are interested in what each woman knows about her own birth, for there is often a connection between how she was born and how she will bring her own child into the world. If, for example, a woman tells us that her mother was under anesthesia and that she was delivered by forceps in a large Parisian hospital, we have reason to expect that her own labor may be difficult. If, on the other hand, she relates that she was born simply, at home, she is more likely to have an easy labor. A woman's daily habits, moreover, have as much influence as her mental attitudes on her experience of giving birth. Women who exercise regularly are better prepared for labor than

those who lead sedentary lives. An expectant mother who is not worn down by stress will also approach labor in better condition.

Obviously, we can't miraculously erase a woman's preconceptions and past experience; but we can create an atmosphere that will encourage women and their partners to approach birth differently. It's especially important that they feel at home in our unit. Women give birth most comfortably surrounded by familiar faces, in a familiar setting—as those who choose to give birth at home well know. At home, of course, not only are the walls and furniture familiar, but so are the noises, smells, and colors. Since, however, hospital deliveries are almost the rule these days, our object is to make the birthplace as much like home as possible. To make the prospective mothers feel at home, we show them around the unit and introduce them to the midwives and assistants who will be present at the delivery. Further, we encourage them to come back as often as they like, and we've designed a whole series of weekly events to interest them in coming. Some women feel a need to come often, even every day. Others come for the first time on the very day they give birth. These women, who seem quite calm about going through labor, tend to be solidly rooted in their own communities and consequently feel less need to participate in events at the hospital before delivery than many of the other, more isolated mothers-to-be. These days, when people no longer speak to each other at the market or on the street, isolation has become a major source of general anxiety. The pregnant woman, especially, needs contact with others; the presence of a supportive community makes her feel happier and more secure. At Pithiviers, we've set aside a large room as a "meeting hall" for just this purpose. Here everyone gets together for discussions, or classes, or just to talk. We purposely leave this room in a state of comfortable disarray. The informal atmosphere puts people at their ease.

Every Thursday night we offer an introduction to Pithiviers. This meeting is usually the first contact a woman or couple has with our clinic. From time to time, people not

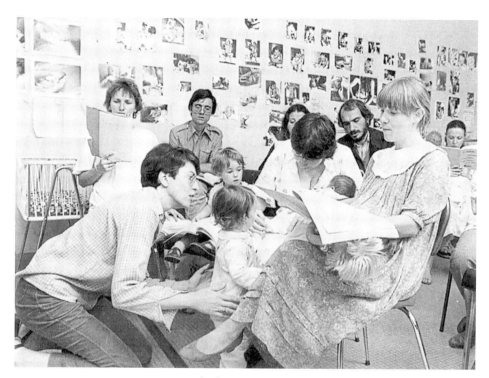

In the meeting room

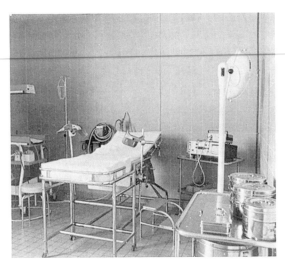

planning to give birth here also attend in search of factual information to help them negotiate an unconventional birth elsewhere. We start with a tour of the premises. After visiting a conventional delivery room, with its solid white walls, bright lights, mysterious electronic machines, and delivery table with bars and stirrups,* we go directly into our "*salle sauvage*," where almost all the babies are actually born at Pithiviers. The contrast between the two rooms is striking. In

the birthing room, the walls are painted in earth tones, the curtains are cream-colored, and the floor is orange. The lights can be dimmed easily. We take care to create a special atmosphere in this room, since the birth process, like all sexual experiences, is heavily influenced by the surrounding environment —by the lighting, the color scheme, the furniture. Moreover, we've removed every piece of furniture that compels any one particular position. When childbirth takes place at home, it is usually in a room with a bed, which strongly suggests a reclining position for labor; in a hospital, the flat table gives a mother no choice but to lie down. In our birthing room, we have a large, low, square cushioned platform on which people can move freely. In harmony with the general look of the room there is a wooden birthing

*The only reason we still have conventional delivery rooms at all is that we form part of a state hospital and are obliged to have the standard equipment. Although we sometimes use the table to stitch up tears, it is never used for delivery. If the alternative birthing room is occupied, it is always possible in any place, even a conventional delivery room, to close the curtains, put a sheet on the floor, introduce extra heating, and very quickly create the right atmosphere.

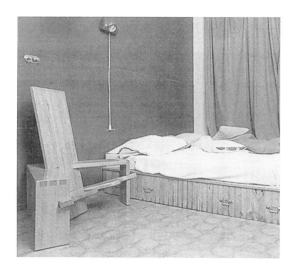

chair, built by a carpenter whose baby was born at Pithiviers. There is also a stereo, a collection of records, and a refrigerator nearby filled with water, fruit juice, and glasses.

In an adjacent room, the atmosphere is completely different, though equally simple. Blues predominate. The azure walls are painted with images evoking ocean waves. Navy blue curtains and a leafy green plant add to the feeling of serenity. In the middle of the room stands a circular, sky-blue pool, custom-made for our needs. We have found that lying in warm water helps women in labor to relax and feel less pain. Seven feet in diameter and two-and-a-half feet deep, the pool easily allows two people freedom of movement. Women can immerse themselves in it completely, without fear.

After this quick tour, there is a general question-and-answer period where we discuss practical, medical, and administrative issues. I always make clear just what we do at Pithiviers to help women in labor and their newborns. People attending this meeting quickly understand that we have almost nothing to teach them in the conventional sense of "childbirth preparation" and that we reject entirely its prescriptive aspects. Above all, we do not teach a "correct" birth position. In opposition to the image so deeply engraved in our minds that all women *must* lie down during labor (in French, the verb for "to labor" and "to give birth," *accoucher*, actually means "to be lying down"), we stress the freedom of the future mother to move as she pleases. We do explain some of the physiological drawbacks of lying down to give birth and assure women that the positions best for them are the ones they find themselves. Nor do we teach breathing techniques. It is impossible to prescribe a breathing method for labor without prescribing a particular birth position; people breathe differently depending on whether they are walking, standing, crouching, kneeling, sitting up, lying down, leaning against something, or floating in water. Our approach is thus in direct conflict with conventional psychoprophylaxis, the Lamaze method, which trains women to control their breathing, their thoughts, and the expression of their emotions. At Pithiviers, I explain, we do just the opposite. On the day of birth, we encourage women in labor to give in to the experience, to lose control, to forget all they have learned—all the cultural images, all the behavioral patterns. The less a woman has learned about the "right" way to have a child, the easier it will be for her.

I also describe a phenomenon typical of the last moments before delivery: a woman entering the final stage of contractions often feels the need to stand up, to flex her knees while hanging onto her partner for support. In preparation for this stage, we do have one thing to teach—though not to the mother: we can teach her partner how to support the shoulders of the woman in labor during her last contractions without getting a backache. The baby's father is usually quite interested in the prospect of such active participation, as are other possible helpers.

Conversations differ greatly from one Thursday to the next. Sometimes questions center on breastfeeding, or the use and efficacy of ultrasound examinations, or the importance of proper diet. Nutrition is becoming a more frequent topic at our Thursday meetings, and rightly so; the crucial nature of dietary habits has been underestimated in the past. Oddly enough, discussions rarely focus on pain. Certainly we talk about the pain of childbirth, but we always emphasize that pain varies from woman to woman and that the very quality of pain changes considerably when a woman does not have to lie on her back, when she can walk around or relax in a pool of warm water. What's more, a woman's attitude towards pain changes as she becomes increasingly confident of her ability to see herself through labor.

I am very insistent that people come to the Thursday meeting only once. First, this is the only way to keep the groups small; second, it prevents the meeting from taking on the qualities of a class. Aside from this one restriction, women and couples are encouraged to come back to the maternity unit whenever they like.

Fridays are devoted to informal conversation. There is no moderator and no set program. Juices and cakes are set out on a table in the middle of the room. It's like a party. People walk around and talk freely among themselves. Mothers holding their babies meet mothers-to-be—always a fruitful encounter. Here again we are far from a teaching mode, yet much information is exchanged at these gatherings and much is learned as people tell each other about the physical and emotional experiences of childbirth.

On Tuesdays we all gather around the piano and sing together. The singing began when we became interested in the question of what a baby can perceive *in utero.* We suspect that the fetus develops a diffuse vibratory sense long before the specialized hearing mechanism of the ear appears. Perhaps very early on, the fetus could perceive sound vibrations, particularly those of its own mother's singing voice, which has a much richer frequency range than her speaking voice.

As time went on, however, we found that the singing group had other, more immediate benefits. For one thing, singing provides a simple way for women to exercise their diaphragm muscles and learn to concentrate on breathing out, which can help them relax during labor. Singing also encourages women to feel comfortable, unself-conscious,

The singing group

and expansive—to experience and release the whole range of emotions. Then, too, the singing group gives expectant women and couples more opportunities to meet new mothers, many of whom still come to sing, their babies in their arms. Other members of the family get to see the birthplace; children are invited to sing with us, and sometimes grandparents come, too. The warmth of these gatherings is difficult to convey. Everyone sings: the midwives sing, and so do I. When we all sing together, the usual separation between consumer and professional dissolves, and a new relationship emerges.

An extraordinary woman by the name of Marie-Louise Aucher animates the singing group with her warm and original personality. Marie-Louise, a professional singer, has devoted much of her life to helping people by teaching them to sing. While conventional music therapy considers individuals only as listeners, Marie-Louise conceives of them as music-makers. (She has worked with chil-

dren and adults, with mental patients and those suffering from Down's syndrome.) At the moment, she is passionately involved in singing with pregnant women at Pithiviers. I first heard about Marie-Louise from mutual friends in 1976. Like us, she was interested in exploring the effects of sound, particularly the mother's voice, on the fetus. One day she came to visit Pithiviers, and I asked her to return on a regular basis. We bought a piano and invited pregnant women to come and sing with her. The singing group has been one of the joys of Pithiviers ever since. Marie-Louise constantly reminds us that we perceive vibrations not only with our ears, but with our whole body. She knows how to bring out the different moods in all of us. On some days she manages to create a sense of quiet calm; on others, an explosion of joyous excitement. Older than the other members of our staff, she sometimes plays the role of grandmother. When she is with us, we truly feel part of a community.

It is common for the singing group to end with dancing, both traditional folk dances and dances like the waltz. The motion involved in dancing may well be beneficial to the fetus's kinesthetic sense, the source of good balance later on. But above all, it is a pleasure to sing and dance. And pleasure must not be underrated; it can only enhance pregnancy.

On Wednesday, a young pediatrician regularly comes to Pithiviers to discuss postnatal

childcare. This open meeting provides yet another chance for the whole family to get to know the clinic, and for pregnant women to be around experienced mothers.

Our "Yoga and Maternity" group on Thursday afternoons is led by a young woman named Gandha, an experienced yoga teacher who had her baby here in 1975. Gandha felt that her knowledge of yoga had helped her during labor and that it would be useful to other women about to give birth. She offered to hold yoga classes at the clinic and I encouraged her to do so. The yoga group was a success and continues to this day. This group is in perfect accord with our philosophy of helping women to discover those physical and emotional resources that will be of use to them during labor and birth and will render medical intervention largely unnecessary. Yoga can help women feel less inhibited, and lead them to use their bodies in seemingly new ways. For instance, through yoga many women rediscover the squatting position which every child knows so well, and which has special benefits for women in labor. Incidentally, the increase in hormonal secretions during pregnancy gives a woman greater physical flexibility and makes these exercises easier to do.

In addition, we encourage women planning to give birth at our clinic to participate in various outside activities. Swimming is highly recommended. In many French cities, public swimming pools have special hours reserved for pregnant women. During this time the water temperature is usually raised to 86°F (30°C) and sometimes a midwife and experienced swimmer will lead the women through various relaxation exercises. Denis Brousse, a swimming instructor from Montpellier, has some particularly interesting ideas to offer to pregnant women. He believes that people who have never learned how to swim are often the most comfortable underwater because they have not yet learned to fight against the sensation of being submerged. Denis encourages the women to learn how to let go, to fall passively into the water, to immerse themselves completely, to make sounds as they breathe out, to touch bottom. These women are able to conquer the panic that pushes them to resurface quickly, and report a sense of strength and well-being. It is a good exercise for overcoming anxiety.

Dearest Papa,

There is one weekly event that I wouldn't skip for the world. I mark the dates down carefully; even without checking my calendar, I haven't missed one yet. And where is it I go? To sing at the maternity clinic. Our dear old Granny, Marie-Louise, is always there, faithful to her work—or, I should say, to her piano. When she opens her mouth to talk to us, one of the most delightful voices I've ever heard fills the room. We all listen attentively, savoring her every word as if it were a delicacy. We are charmed, captivated, overwhelmed. When she sits down at the piano, notes drop like pearls. Her voice rings out, singing for all the unborn babies and the mothers who carry them. With the simplicity of a true artist, she manages to take us all to the opera!

When singing "La flute et la belle eau," we are totally unaware of how high we are climbing until we're well up into the clouds, sitting on high B-flat. How did we get so high, and then sweep down to the ground again without getting hurt? All of a sudden, Marie-Louise is talking with one of the little ones. She always has a gentle word to

put in, a sweet thought for the children, for all the fresh voices ready to sing. She adjusts her glasses on her nose, and she's off again, into the celestial spheres of nursery rhymes and lullabies. Froggy's gone a courtin' and Little Muskrat a-tat-tat a-tat-tat has come to sing and dance with Big Rat. Or Old Mother Hubbard has gone to the cupboard, and the Man in the Moon comes to give us a flick with his long tooth-pick-stick!

Still smiling, she moves on to more serious subjects: true love, blue love, the world of grown-ups. Sailors board ships for the lands of their dreams and will not be forgotten. Love borders on pain borders on love, and the bluebird of happiness sings tender moments into our lives.

Abruptly, Marie-Louise steps up the rhythm. The melodies move faster and faster. We hurry along at an unrelenting pace, but where to, nobody knows. Phew! you need a deep breath after a song like that! Marie-Louise gets up. Her mischievous eyes are twinkling behind the glint of her glasses. We are all warmed by the smile of a sparkling spirit, the poetry of childhood, the happiness of living with her words and her music. In a flash, she is asking us to dance, to clear away the chairs, to float freely in the melodies of her guitar. And soon we are all dancing.

One day Marie-Louise was in even better spirits than usual. I was curious and asked her why. Her answer was simple: "I've just come from court. My neighbor clogged up all my drainpipes, and the situation is so ridiculous that it's put me in the most marvelous mood!" Well, I could see her point. When you sing, life sings, and nothing can stop the bubbling stream of joy inside you.

Marie-Louise is so young, it's hard to believe how old she really is. She has seen seventy-two springtimes open their blossoms, but her heart is eternally young. You would love her, Papa— fiddler that you are!

Your loving daughter

Though a woman's daily activities play a significant role in preparing her for birth, prenatal medical care has an important influence on the progress of labor and birth. In France today, prenatal examinations are compulsory during the third, sixth, eighth, and ninth months. Some doctors and women find it useful to schedule additional check-ups. In any case, it is the style and not the number of prenatal examinations that appears to determine the nature of their influence.

All too often such consultations treat pregnancy as an illness. The routine course of these sessions frequently leads to more problems than it solves. To begin with, the prenatal visit usually brings to light some potentially worrisome element on which the doctor will undoubtedly focus: the cervix is too short, too soft, or half-open; the baby is too large or too small for its gestational age; the mother has gained too much weight or not enough; her blood pressure is too high or too low; the shape or size of her pelvis is unfavorable; and so on. An ultrasound examination usually follows, providing the doctor with yet another chance to discover some upsetting detail about the position of the placenta, or the size and shape of the fetus. Finally, there are so many blood and urine tests that results of at least one of them are bound to fall outside the "normal" range. A consultation of this type usually ends with the doctor prescribing some kind of medication, and sometimes even bedrest.

There is a second type of consultation, which might be called neutral and which must often undo the effects of this first type. At Pithiviers, we aim for examinations of this second kind. The check-up can be very brief; a skilled doctor really needs very little time to grasp the essentials. The first step is to check for any anomalies that demand immediate action. In fact, however, there are very few cases where it is useful or even possible to act on a problematic diagnosis. Urinary tract infections can be treated, and hospitalization is advisable when protein deposits in the urine, a sudden rise in blood pressure, and edema indicate a positive diagnosis of pre-eclampsia—a stage of toxemia, and a major cause of fatality in pregnant women. We may also suggest that a woman working at a tiring and unfulfilling job take some time off, if she can arrange to receive benefits during her leave.*

We request only the most rudimentary urine and blood tests, and we rarely use ultrasound examinations. This surprises both doctors and expectant mothers alike, because use of ultrasound in the majority of clinics and hospitals has by now become routine. People, in fact, seem to ascribe almost magical qualities to these tests, believing they will

*In France, a woman can leave her job and still get paid from six to eight weeks before birth to ten weeks after. Furthermore, a doctor can prescribe rest at any time, and the French national insurance will subsidize the leave.

solve all sorts of possible problems. Certainly an ultrasound examination can provide a great deal of information to satisfy the curiosity of parents and doctors alike. Ultimately, however, it only rarely tells us more than the diagnosis of a skilled doctor. Even when such an examination does tell us something we could not have discovered by other methods, we have found it seldom leads us to a procedural change.

For example, let us suppose that an early ultrasound shows the placenta to be attached too low in the uterus. This finding may cause a woman great anxiety, yet there is nothing the doctor can do about it until the birth. Furthermore, it makes no sense to worry about it, since placental placement becomes important only near the end of pregnancy—when most such placentas tend to move away from the cervix in any case. During labor, it is easy for a skilled practitioner to check manually that the placenta is not in the way. If, indeed, it does cover the entire cervical opening, then he can advise a cesarean. If it covers the opening only partially, labor may continue, with intervention held in reserve as an option if the mother loses too much blood, or the fetus is endangered in any way.

Take another common occurence—ultrasound reveals a twin pregnancy early on. Regardless of the results of the test, however, sometimes only one fetus will continue to develop. Instead of depending on this exam, all one need do is wait patiently until the seventh or eighth month of pregnancy, when the practitioner can easily detect twins during a thorough external examination. Sometimes ultrasound can pick up neural-tube malformations such as anencephaly or spina bifida. For this discovery to be of practical value, however, it must be made early enough to allow a voluntary interruption of pregnancy. An ultrasonographer can never be 100 percent certain of such diagnoses, making the issue of whether or not to have an abortion even more problematic. In any case, it should be emphasized that many babies with neural-tube defects are destined to die of natural causes *in utero,* or within a few days of birth. Another frequent reason for the use of ultrasound is to confirm the precise date of conception, and thus the due date. Yet even when the expectant mother has had irregular periods, an experienced practitioner can almost always fix the date just as accurately by asking the right kinds of questions and examining the woman early in pregnancy.

For the most part, ultrasound findings, however interesting, are useless for all practical purposes. At Pithiviers it is a general rule to perform such supplementary examinations only when they will have a definite effect on a doctor's or pregnant woman's decisions, and this general rule leaves us with very few occasions to use ultrasound.

Aside from this principle of keeping intervention to a minimum, there are other good reasons for limiting the use of ultrasound. It is important to remember that we have no way of knowing at this time how ultrasound exposure, even for very short times, might affect the mother—or the fetus. Although many physicians and ultrasound technicians believe the procedure is harmless, large-scale studies are under way investigating its effects on genetic make-up, fetal development, hematological and vascular conditions, the immune system, and much more.[2] Because this research has just begun, it is too early to arrive at definite conclusions. We can only wait and wonder about what we will see forty years from now, when one or two generations will have been literally rocked *in utero* by sonic waves.

Another controversial prenatal test is amniocentesis. This consists of using ultrasound to determine the position of the fetus, and then inserting a needle through the mother's abdominal wall to obtain a sample of amniotic fluid. This fluid contains cast-off fetal cells which are grown in culture until it is possible to determine their chromosomal composition. Amniocentesis is usually done at about sixteen weeks' gestation, and results are available after about three weeks. It has become common for women over thirty-five to have amniocentesis, since, as a woman gets older, she runs a greater risk of having a child with Down's syndrome.

At Pithiviers, we keep an open mind about amniocentesis. In some exceptional cases where there is a history of genetic disease in the family, amniocentesis might indeed relieve a woman's fears and help her feel more at ease. But in most cases, regardless of a woman's age, we never urge that she undergo this test. We do, however, provide her with as much information as possible so that she can calculate the risks involved and decide for herself. She must understand that amniocentesis is useful only if, in the light of abnormal results, she would consider having an abortion, and that the procedure itself involves a risk of miscarriage in the neighborhood of 0.5 to 2 percent. Certain studies also suggest a greater incidence of respiratory difficulties for the newborn and a correlation with a higher rate of orthopedic malformations if the mother has had amniocentesis in the second trimester. We also encourage her to interpret statistics within a positive framework. For instance, instead of saying that women of forty run a 1-in-109 risk of having a Down's syndrome child, why not consider that such women have about a 99 percent chance of having a genetically healthy child? Our aim is to inform, never to frighten. As a result, we find that many women at Pithiviers choose to forego amniocentesis.[3]

Finally, our way of dealing with the risk of premature birth does not conform in the least with popular doctrines of the past several years. A veritable obsession with prematurity has led many doctors to advocate an aggressive preventive attitude. In many countries, bedrest is commonly prescribed to guard against premature labor, yet not one study has been able to demonstrate that bedrest has any such effect. We therefore remain quite skeptical about the effectiveness of such a prescription. This policy against bedrest is also motivated by our worry that prolonged immobilization may lead to fetal sensory deprivation by limiting input to the vestibular organ—the inner part of the ear—which processes information on the body's position and eventually ensures proper balance. In addition, the vestibular organ possibly affects the fetus's orientation *in utero,* and deficiencies in its function might result in breech or shoulder presentations. From our point of view, the common prescription of bedrest can only be viewed as yet another example of the intrusion of obstetrics into the birth process: women are told to lie down not just during labor, but for the whole of pregnancy as well.

Along these same lines, we also question the practice of prescribing drugs that inhibit uterine contractions to prevent premature birth. First, these drugs—which women may take for days, weeks, even months—have intense, adverse side effects such as palpitations, dizziness, and overall malaise. If a woman comes to us concerned about feeling uterine contractions, we first establish that she is not going into labor. Then we point out that the uterus is a muscle, not an inert container; contractions exercise and strengthen the uterine muscles and may provide stimulation that the baby needs. If a woman complains that these contractions are painful, a warm bath may well relieve her discomfort. Second, we fear that these drugs may inhibit the awakening or proper development of fetal sensory functions. We are particularly troubled by the contention of some physicians that they can determine whether or not a child gestated under the influence of such drugs by testing its skin sensitivity after birth.

Finally, it is unusual for us to perform cerclage. Cerclage consists of sewing the cervix closed, and may be done as early as the third month of pregnancy. More common in France than in the United States or England, cerclage is indicated to remedy a condition of the cervix whereby it opens prematurely. The diagnosis of "incompetent cervix" is, however, very subjective. Moreover, premature labor is rarely related to the condition of the cervix. In hospitals where cerclage is common, the prematurity rate is not significantly lower than in other places where it is seldom performed. As I tell pregnant women, it is not the cervix that determines when labor actually begins, but rather the baby itself.

Most European countries now have a prematurity rate of 6 percent or 7 percent, which constitutes a slight decline from preceding years. This downward trend in premature births since the 1970s has been directly attributed to the aggressive medical approach involving more frequent prenatal examinations, advanced technology, and the prescription of new drugs. But there may be other reasons for the decline. At our clinic, where the opposite attitudes prevail, of the 1,000 births before December 31, 1973, 4.9 percent were premature; of the 1,000 births before December 31, 1980, 2.5 percent were premature.* The recent and continued decline in our already low rate might be explained by the fact that, over the last decade,

women coming to Pithiviers have become more economically privileged as a group, which means they tend to be in better physical health and thus less likely to go into labor prematurely. The statistical differential between our figures and the world at large is, however, far too great to be attributed solely to this factor. Perhaps an alternative correlation could be established between our low prematurity rate and our general style of prenatal care.

Sometimes we can't help wondering whether pregnant women wouldn't get more out of coming to sing with us than from going to yet another prenatal examination.

*For the sake of simplicity, we call "premature" all babies weighing less than 5.5 pounds at birth.

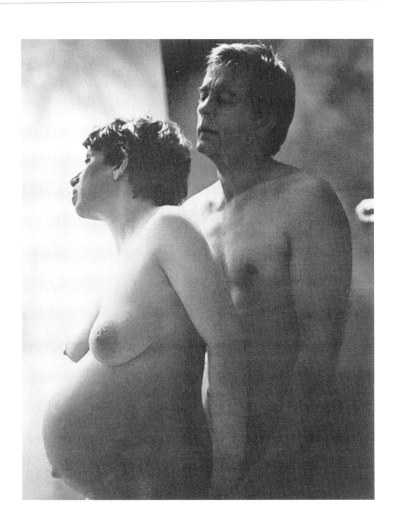

helping women in labor

A woman in labor arrives at the clinic. Her first contact with the midwife is important; the midwife's kindly look, smile, words, and gestures all have a beneficial effect on labor. Decisions made at this time can also be significant. For instance, an experienced midwife will be able to determine the precise stage of labor. If it has just begun, the midwife might advise the woman to wait before coming to the clinic—perhaps to take a walk, or even go home for a while if she lives nearby. If a woman goes back to familiar surroundings and stays active, it is likely that when she returns to the clinic, labor will be well advanced. If a woman stays in the clinic during the whole first stage of labor—the stage when the cervix is gradually dilating—we assist her, but not in any preconceived way; we have learned from experience not to be mechanical or dogmatic. Every woman is different, and it follows that each labor will be different. We accept this. We do not plan particular strategies, nor do we adopt hard-and-fast rules.

This does not interfere with close teamwork: having worked together for some time now, we are often able to communicate with merely a glance or a gesture. Nor does it mean that we have no general procedures; on the contrary, several have evolved naturally over the years, in harmony with our commitment to flexibility, innovation, and the central importance of the mother. These general guidelines are equally suited to all women, regardless of their past histories, and apply whether a woman has visited the clinic regularly or has first come to us at the height of active labor. These general guidelines apply to women we know well, and to women we have scarcely met; to workers and intellectuals; to city women and country women; to native-born and foreign women.

To begin with, at Pithiviers we want to destroy the image of the pregnant woman as patient that is so deeply ingrained in Western culture. We discourage the woman entering the hospital from promptly putting on her nightgown and climbing into bed. The first stage of labor may take place in the bedroom, in the large meeting room, or in the birthing room. During this time, some women choose to walk through the corridors or stroll in the garden. At Pithiviers we stress that anything is possible.

Woman in labor strolling with friends

As first-stage labor advances and contractions become more intense, it feels best for the mother to move into a calm, dimly lit place. The woman, listening to her own body, needs to concentrate and is apt to find external distractions intrusive. A serene environment can ease a woman's transition into her own inner world. Many mammals, after all, give birth in dark, quiet, out-of-the-way corners. It is not surprising, then, that human beings also seek out such settings for labor and birth. Our *"salle sauvage"* is designed to fulfill this need. Ideally, all sensory stimulation should be reduced. In some cases, low, soothing music enhances the feeling of calm and quietude. The room is warm enough for a woman to feel comfortable without her clothes. Most remove their glasses or contact lenses, to focus inward more completely.

The woman in labor is urged to trust what she feels, to move as she pleases, to take any position she finds spontaneously. She can walk, sit, kneel, lean on someone or something, or lie down if she feels like it. Given such freedom, women rarely choose dorsal or semi-seated positions for long periods of time, because they are simply not comfortable. For the same reason, most naturally avoid lying on their backs toward the end of pregnancy and prefer instead to curl up on their sides. If a woman in labor is on her back and hesitates to move around or change positions, we sometimes succumb to the temptation to explain to her that this position

restricts oxygen transfer to the baby because it interferes with blood flow to the uterus by compressing the aorta and the vena cava.

This explanation is usually unnecessary, since most women in the early phases of labor instinctively prefer to stand bent forward, leaning on a piece of furniture, or to get down on their hands and knees.* It is not by chance that so many women find this position spontaneously and hold it for a long time; it effectively reduces pain, especially backaches. In addition, it is a sort of physical folding inward that makes it easier for a woman to ignore external distractions. (This position resembles the posture of prayer, which itself is a transition to a different state of consciousness.) Kneeling also seems to play an important role from a mechanical point of view. In the case of posterior presentations, which often cause the longest and most difficult labors, it facilitates rotation of the baby's head in the pelvis. Since the heaviest part of the infant's body is its back, the baby will tend to turn toward the front of the uterus when the woman is on all fours. In summary, walking, kneeling, sitting, standing, leaning on someone or something are the most common basic labor positions, but each has countless individual variations.

*When the woman is on all fours, one leg is usually higher, or one side further forward, than the other. Because the baby's head has to make a spiral in the pelvis, birth is by nature an asymmetrical phenomenon. This is yet another reason why the symmetrical supine position is inappropriate.

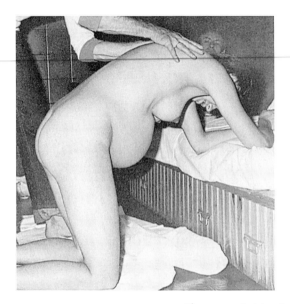
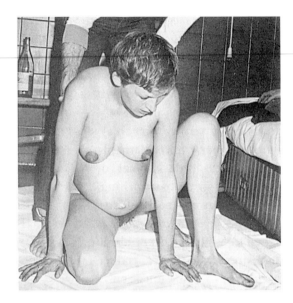

The woman in labor is free to take any position
she finds spontaneously . . .

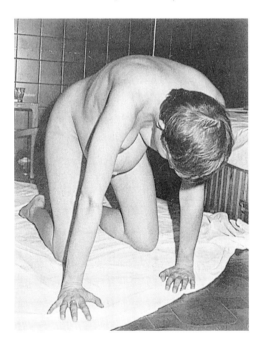

The midwives see to the basics—they make sure that the room is warm, dark, and quiet, and that each woman feels free to change positions at will. They offer water, fruit juice, honey, and sugar, which provide women with the fluids and calories they need to do the hard work of childbirth. It is easy enough to teach others how to follow these steps of our routine. But helping a woman in labor involves much more than these simple tasks. It involves empathy, intuition, and inspiration; it is an art.

It is the intuitive sense that enables a midwife to "feel out" whether people present during labor are playing positive or negative roles. Women in labor often want to have someone they know nearby, and seem to need to establish a special relationship with at least one person during labor. In our society, this person is often the baby's father. It may not always be best, however, for a woman to have her partner there. Certain men have a beneficial presence, while others only slow labor down. Sometimes an over-anxious man will get worried and will then try to hide it by talking too much; his chatter can keep the woman from concentrating on her labor. I think of one incident, when a woman couldn't seem to get beyond eight centimeters' dilation; when her husband left the room for a short time to rest, their baby was born. Though this woman had told us that she wanted her husband present, her body was saying the reverse. A particularly overprotective and possessive man can also

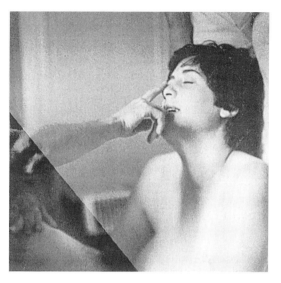

Tenderness matters more than technique

have a negative effect on labor. He continuously massages, caresses, and holds *his* woman, who belongs to *him*. He anticipates her demands rather than responds to them. The woman in labor requires calm, but he can provide only stimulation. Men sometimes find it hard to observe, accept, and understand a woman's instinctive behavior during childbirth. Instead, they often try to keep her from slipping out of a rational, self-controlled state. It is not mere coincidence that in all traditional societies, women in labor are assisted not by men, but by other women who have had children themselves.

Some mothers-to-be prefer to bring a sister or female friend to the clinic. If the friend or sister has had a spontaneous natural birth herself, she will bring her positive knowledge of the experience to the event; if she has never had children, or if she has had only cesarean births, she may well bring fear and anxiety. Other women prefer to have several people with them at the clinic. We have noticed that many of these women have long and difficult labors. One night while the midwives and I were watching television, we saw a big car pull up outside. A pregnant woman, apparently in labor, stepped out of the car, followed by a man, a woman, a very young girl, and another man with a camera. The first reaction from the midwives was, "Well, looks like we're in for a long night." They were right: the labor was long and drawn-out. Perhaps certain women want to be surrounded by people at this time because of some underlying fear or insecurity about labor. Yet these anxious feelings may become even stronger if the woman in labor senses that she is being watched or feels she must play some specific role in relation to those present. On the other hand, women from tight-knit families or communities are often comforted during labor by the presence of the people they are used to seeing every day.

Occasionally a woman will come to the clinic with her own mother. This can be very helpful if the mother has had a number of children without medical intervention, but such is not often the case for mothers who gave birth in the fifties and sixties. Much that mothers experienced in childbirth then is now outdated. In addition, the medical practices surrounding birth are still changing very quickly, so that it can be difficult for mothers to pass on valuable and valid information to their daughters as they do in traditional societies. The resulting gap in experience and knowledge explains some of the tensions we have observed between mothers and daughters. In many cases, this gap can be filled most effectively by the companionship of an experienced and empathetic midwife.

The importance of midwives cannot be exaggerated. Regardless of particular obstetrical practices, more women have normal labors and births wherever midwives presently play a major role in childbirth, whether it be in Ireland, in The Netherlands, or here at Pithiviers. It is very important that midwives be women—a truth that is apparently not as obvious as it seems, since midwifery schools in countries such as France, Sweden, and the United Kingdom have started admitting men. Labor, birth, and breastfeeding are in part sexual events, and the gender of those people present must be taken into account. The contact between the birth attendant and the woman in labor can be exceedingly intimate and intense. A woman in labor is in an especially vulnerable physical and emotional state, apt to become dependent on her birth attendant, at least for a while. The sexual overtones that might accompany such contact with a male attendant could hamper the woman in labor in acting as openly and spon-

Woman with midwife in the "salle sauvage"

taneously as she would like, or afterwards might even make her feel ashamed of what she has revealed about herself. Of course, it's not that simple. For all the importance of gender, the essential quality a birth attendant —male or female—must have is the ability to help a woman feel secure and at ease.

To sum up, privacy, intimacy, calm, freedom to labor in any position, and the helpful presence of midwives are crucial to a spontaneous first-stage labor. The harsh lighting, sudden noises, cold machines, and masked intruders typical of modern hospital environments, along with the absence of midwives, the denial or ignorance of their importance, and the confinement of women in labor to restricted positions—all inhibit labor.

Yet even when a woman is in the most favorable atmosphere, dilation sometimes stops and contractions become more painful and less efficient. At this point, a warm bath can often provide some relief. There are now two small pools at the clinic which we use for this purpose. The woman immerses herself in warm water, often up to her neck. Sometimes an attentive hand gently supports her head while her ears are submerged. In the pool, labor becomes easier, more comfortable, less painful, and more efficient. For one thing, water makes a woman weightless; she can float and no longer has to fight against the weight of her own body during contractions. Furthermore, the warmth of the water reduces adrenaline secretion and relaxes the muscles. Water can also induce alpha brain waves, creating a state of mental relaxation. And relaxation, in turn, brings on quick dilation. On occasion, when a labor is not progressing, the turn of the faucet, the sight and sound of running water, will bring on birth before the pool is full!

We tend to reserve our pools for women who have painful and inefficient contractions at around five centimeters' dilation. But water can be relaxing for the others, too. It can be as comforting as a lover, a mother, or a midwife. The affinity of pregnant women for water is still a mystery to us. Many mothers-to-be say that they are drawn to water; they feel a strong urge to dive into the waves, or dream of floating on the surface for long periods of time. Some women who are strongly drawn to water throughout pregnancy are even more attracted to it during labor. Still others tell us that they don't like the water or can't swim. Yet as labor begins, these same women will suddenly move to-

ward the pool, enter eagerly, and not want to leave!

As the first stage of labor nears its end, a woman usually does get out of the pool. She feels the need to become more active, to help the baby emerge. Often, at this point, the woman may have a distant look in her eyes, even seem to be in a different world; if she speaks at all, she will repeat single words or simple sentences. These are all signs to us that she is responding to what is instinctive within herself and that she has attained a good hormonal balance. Far from considering her state irrational and helpless, we are then quite sure that she knows best what to do to help her child come into the world.

Our way of determining the onset of second-stage labor—when the dilation of the cervix is complete—is quite different from common medical practice. Most physicians do a vaginal examination to decide whether a woman should start to push or not. We can usually distinguish between stages of labor without internal exams—which should in any event be kept to a minimum. We know that second-stage labor has begun when a woman who has been standing or walking around suddenly wants to bend her knees during contractions and has an urgent need to grasp something or someone. If she and her partner are standing face to face in each others' arms, she will hang from his neck during contractions. Should her partner be standing behind her, she may squat as he lends support under her arms. The woman

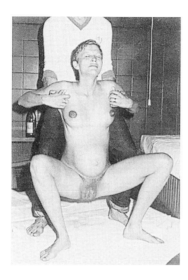

lets herself go; as she cries out, with her vulva wide open and her legs spread apart, it seems as if her entire body is opening up at once. She may even get to the point where she releases her sphincter muscles and empties her rectum. The release of these muscles, and her strong, typical cry, go against the most deeply embedded social behavior. They tell us that the woman in labor has entered the optimum instinctive state of consciousness; in other words, she has achieved the right hormonal balance.

Most women at Pithiviers give birth in supported squatting positions, by far the most efficient from a mechanical point of view, since they maximize downward weight, minimize muscular effort and oxygen consumption, and facilitate relaxation of the perineal muscles. The attendant can feel a contraction coming on by placing her right hand over the top of a woman's uterus. When the contraction begins, the attendant will usually slide her hands under the woman's armpits in order to hold her hands or clasp her thumbs. He or she stands up straight without leaning forward, becoming a kind of human backrest. If a woman labors in the squatting position, two people can hold her at once: one who is experienced and one who is close to the woman but new to the situation and perhaps hesitant. But a woman may also choose to face her partner and hang from his neck, with her legs wide apart. This position, in which the woman's feet are at moments off the ground, is also extraordinarily useful. It relaxes the abdominal and perineal muscles assisting the baby's descent. The person holding the woman cannot help pressing lightly against her abdomen, and so makes it easier for her to hold her legs apart.

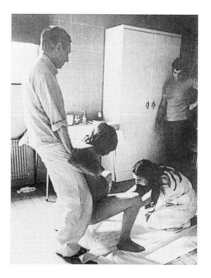

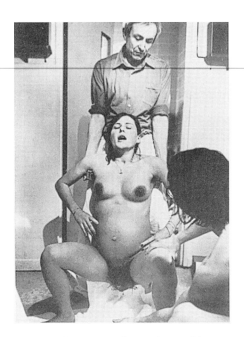

Birth in the supported squatting position . . .

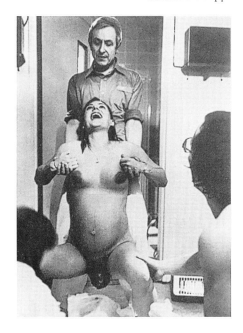

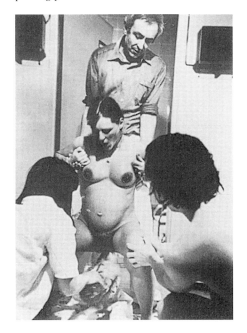

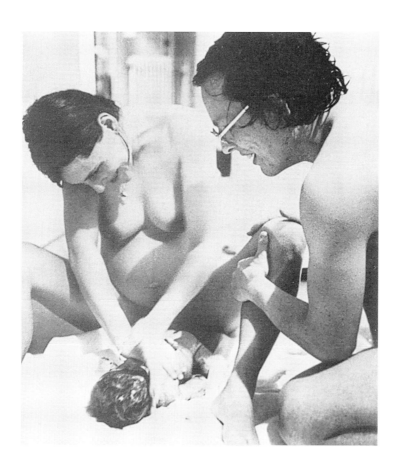

Though squatting and hanging are the common second-stage labor positions at our clinic, they are by no means the rule. A woman is free to find any position conducive to her comfort and relaxation. She may adopt a variety of asymmetrical positions, sitting with one leg straight out or leaning sideways; she may want to lie down, stretch out on her side, sit on a chair, or get down on all fours. (Note that this last position is much like the squatting position—if you let go of a woman who is squatting, she will fall forward onto her hands and knees.) She may even give birth in the water, an interesting new development that has resulted from our use of pools. Sometimes women are so relaxed in the pools that they are reluctant to emerge from the water, even when they feel labor progressing quickly. Here, too, women seem to know that it is not at all dangerous to give birth in water; there is no risk to the newborn, who, after all, has known only watery environments. A baby will start to breathe air through its lungs only after it comes to the surface of the water and suddenly feels the difference in atmosphere and temperature for the first time. We have never made a point of having babies born under water, but this unexpected event does happen several times a month (twenty to thirty times a year).

Birth in the water . . .

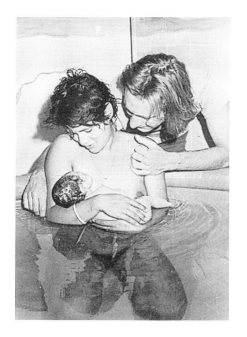

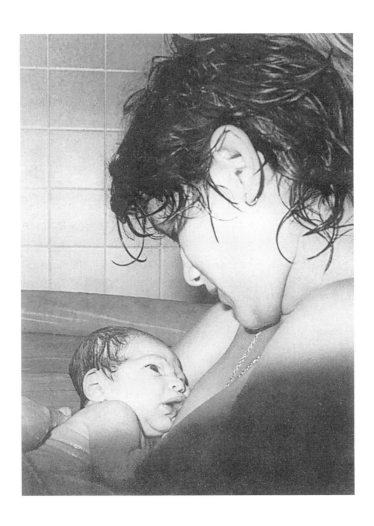

Whatever position a woman finds, we have noticed that in helping her, tenderness is just as important as technique. Experienced, empathetic attendants are able to sense a woman's feelings of calm, tension, or fear from the texture and dampness of her skin. Body to body, skin to skin, a midwife will rely on touching and holding a woman, rather than speaking to her. When she does speak, she will use simple words, words a young child could understand. This ideal communion does not exclude a degree of firmness in certain situations. For instance, if a woman in labor feels sleepy just before the last two or three contractions, the attendant should encourage her to remain active. It's important then to say something like, "It's too late to postpone the birth, it's time. . . ." Words, however, are usually irrelevant at times like this, and certain words—like "push" or "harder"—can actually have definite negative effects. Most often the woman in childbirth knows exactly what she is feeling, and certain instructions may only conflict with her experience. I tend not to say anything. If I do speak, it will be something like "Good . . . good . . . let the baby come . . . ." If the woman seems gripped by the fear of failure, I might suggest, "Don't push, don't push," or "Don't hold back, cry, shout, if you want to."

These are our ways of helping women to give birth at Pithiviers. The strategies and techniques identified with us have an important part to play, but our aim is much broader. We want to enable *all* women, in *any* position, to give birth with confidence.

A mother from Latin America

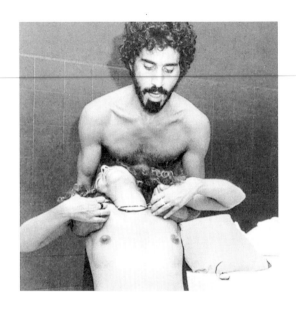

They say that during the last few hours before birth, you lose contact with the outside world. This was true for me. I found myself in another universe, on a distant planet, drifting in a sea of sensations.

It was a very strange night. People were sleeping. And there we were, the whole night through, Philippe and I, and the other couple, awake, between the bedroom and the birthing room. The other couple had their baby at about five in the morning. We were stunned by the vivid image of them returning in the darkness with a child in their arms. It was reassuring to know that a woman could give birth and then walk out on her own two feet. We were comforted.

At some point, the contractions began to get sharper, more violent. I clutched Philippe, then the piano, then Philippe again. The room became a sequence of comings and goings. The pain became difficult to control. It was part of me, it had no end, no beginning. When Dr. Odent arrived, I was reaching out to the midwife, who seemed very far from me. I could not understand the endless pain.

And that's when I became one with the sea. The pain moved to a new place, it was duller. Nuria, our baby, was there. I could feel her, inch by inch, slowly making her way out. It felt so good to let my body go in this sea of sensations, to close my eyes and let the waves gently rock me. One day, in a tiny village in India, I passed an old man dressed in white. He sat on a doorstep, his hands folded in prayer. As I passed, he lifted his head towards me. To say hello? To bless me with peace? I walked softly and answered him with the same gesture. This incident and the sea are interwoven among the infinite strands of space and time which mark Nuria's birth.

I sometimes ask Philippe to sit down and tell me what actually happened, what he saw, since my memory is one of another world.

A mother from Paris

The most comfortable position for me was kneeling on the floor, with my chest leaning over an armchair. When Dr. Odent walked in, I was in such pain that I burst into tears. I saw him leave without saying a word. He soon came back with a woman of about twenty in a white smock, a student nurse who stayed close to me from then on. When I felt the next contraction, I threw myself into her arms, and a strong bond began to grow between us. I felt her warmth, her gentleness. Together we went into a birthing room. At each contraction, I would hold her tightly until the pain had subsided. I will always be grateful for all she

gave me. Earlier, when I was alone in my room, I had tried to "control the pain" by means of deep-breathing exercises. The nurse's comforting presence brought a noticeable change: I no longer tried to control myself. I screamed at each contraction. My cries didn't stop until an hour and fifteen minutes later, when the baby was born.

These cries amazed me. With my first child, I hadn't felt any desire to scream or cry. Now I had the impression that I was rousing the entire hospital. Never in my life had I wailed like that before. It was as if the cries didn't belong to me. When my husband arrived, just before delivery, I reassured him: "Don't worry, I can't help it, it feels good to scream, sit down." At one point I heard myself crying out in a different way: long, trembling howls, like the cries of a baby. I realize now that these cries protected me, not from the pain, but from a traumatic inscription of this pain on my psyche. It was a kind of catharsis; by screaming, I let the pain leave my body.

Near the end of my labor, I began to curse. I can't remember what I said: I had lost control of my senses. That experience has outlived the actual moment of birth. To think that I could act like this in front of other people! Yet it was as if, after losing my own voice for so many years, I had finally found it again.

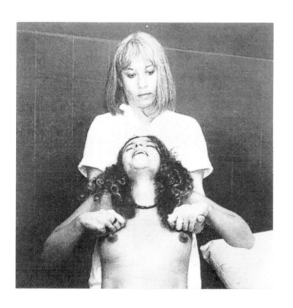

A mother from Leeds

Monday, December seventh. Eddie had to hurry breakfast. Thirty miles of very straight, very flat, treelined road through the French countryside, rushing to Pithiviers. The poetry escapes me; the contractions were coming every fifteen trees....

The midwife examines me: it will probably be today, this afternoon. That seems a long time away; it is only ten o'clock. We are very excited. The pain is getting more insistent. After a while, the contractions begin, coming fast and furious. My legs seem to give way a lot. I lie down on one of the couches in the meeting room. For a second I have a doubt; why didn't I have an epidural? Then I would not be going through this pain. It seems I can't take it—it's too much all at once; I am no heroine. I start screaming and that helps. The pain is still there, stronger every time, but the screaming makes it bearable. I suddenly bury my head in Eddie's jacket, which lies on the couch. His smell is there. He is there, too, but with the pain so strong, I don't want him to touch me. Strangely enough, he is calm. It is ten past eleven. I ask Eddie to go and get somebody; the pain is too great. The midwife and Dr. Odent arrive, serene and reassuring. The dilation is complete, to their

surprise and my relief. Dr. Odent speaks of blue waters and beaches; they start filling the pool.

With Eddie and Dr. Odent at my side, I walk to the birth room. The sun is streaming through the windows. Dr. Odent is humming quietly. In the birth room, I undress. The room is semi-dark: brown tiling on the walls, a warm-colored floor, and a big platform with multihued cushions and a big birthing chair. I am grateful for the quiet; your senses can only take so much at a time.

In only ten minutes, I feel a tremendous urge to push. The midwife is there instantly, amazed at the speed of my labor's progress. I am breathing like a toad: through the top of my throat. Dr. Odent comes in. The waters break. The midwife gently suggests that I adopt a semi-squatting position, supported by Eddie. At first I am not too sure, but it does help. As each contraction overwhelms me, I am still moaning very loud, but just for the length of the contraction. Everyone else is calm, quiet, and supportive. Dr. Odent gives me lumps of sugar, for energy, and water (I drink about two pints in all). Suddenly I can feel the head coming down. I am glad because I am looking forward to sleeping, baby or no baby. While standing between contractions, I rock on my feet very gently. The head is visible. Eddie is supporting me.

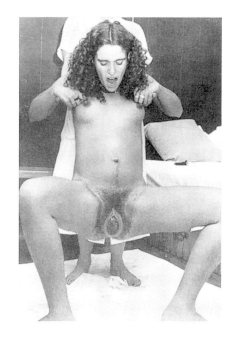
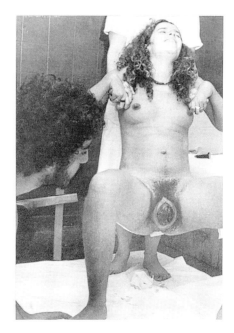

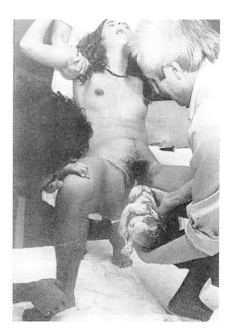

One push and I feel our baby coming out. The midwife catches her, I think she helped turn her slightly. My memory of that second is hazy with excitement.

Eddie lowers me and they put the baby in my arms. I am stunned: not a word is spoken. The baby cries a bit and starts looking for the nipple.

All is so peaceful and so intense. The midwife and Dr. Odent are in a corner, available, yet making themselves totally unobtrusive. The moment belongs to the three of us. Somebody brings a bath (filled from the pool I did not have time to get into). Camille, our daughter, still attached to me, unfolds in the water.

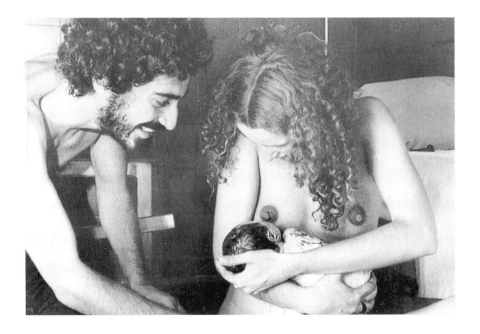

the first hour and after

There are many who feel that the first hour after birth is a very important time for newborns and mothers alike. It may determine, in part, how children relate to their mothers, which in turn could affect how they will approach other people and the world around them. This critical period after birth may well influence a person's capacity for loving, and for attachment in general. We therefore take special care to provide a warm and reassuring climate that fosters intimacy between mother and child at this time.

As I have described, most women at Pithiviers give birth in the supported squatting position. Midwives at our clinic do not touch the perineum or hold the baby's head as it comes out. After the infant's head appears and rotates on its own, the birth attendant must sometimes gently help the shoulders emerge. More often, the child's whole body slides out by itself and the attendant's task is simply to keep the baby from landing on the floor. After birth the mother, who was squatting until then, simply sits down on the floor. Many women spontaneously sit up with their backs straight at this point. Once the

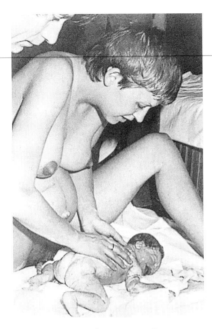

The "safety position"

mother is sitting, we place the baby between her knees in a "safety position," that is, on its stomach with its head turned to the side. This way, even if the baby has some liquid in its mouth and lacks, as yet, efficient reflexes to protect its respiratory tract, gravity prevents such fluid from flowing back into the lungs. The baby lies in this position for only a few seconds, just long enough to let out a vigorous cry, take some deep breaths, cough or sneeze, pink up, and show good body tone. The room is well heated, but if necessary we will cover the baby with a blanket. Then, the mother takes the child into her arms. The two are still attached by the umbil-

ical cord, and the mother's upright position makes their connection as rich and complete as possible. Every part of the baby's body is in contact with its mother. The two look at each other almost immediately; the intensity of this moment is felt by everyone present. The mother often responds to her baby's cries with affectionate sounds and simple words: their dialogue begins. The father, if present, is generally overcome with emotion, and often in tears. The family camera will most likely be forgotten in a corner, unless the midwife thinks to take pictures.

There is no clock in the birthing room. We take our time. No one ever thinks to record the exact moment of birth—unless the parents are interested in astrology and ask us to note the precise second of their child's first breath. Busy professionals, impatient to get on to something else, often try to hurry this period after birth. For us, however, this is a most precious time. There is nothing to lose, and so much to gain, by letting a mother and her child get to know each other at their leisure.

For one thing, we know that prolonged skin-to-skin contact and, in particular, the baby's suckling, coupled with the intense emotions felt at this time, actually stimulate a woman's hormonal secretions. These secretions in turn cause further contractions that are necessary to expel the placenta spontaneously. The placenta may come out at the first moment of contact between mother and baby, or not for thirty minutes or more.

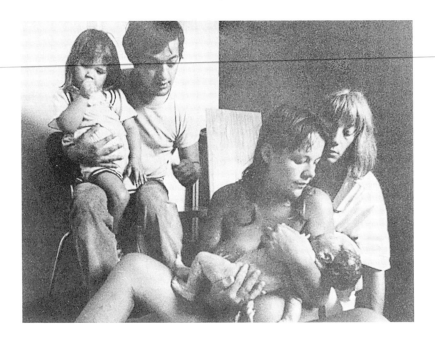

There is no point in rushing. It is more important that the placenta detach easily than that it emerge quickly; the less hurry, the less risk of hemorrhage. When a woman feels contractions signaling the detachment of the placenta, she will naturally focus less on the baby for a few moments. She may want to lie down, keeping her baby in her arms; if so, it is best for her to lie on her left side so as not to compress the vena cava. She may also take the supported squatting position again, usually during a contraction. It is occasionally useful to put pressure just above the pubic bone in order to check whether the placenta has detached (if the cord does not move back up, the placenta is ready for delivery). But

this causes pain and discomfort to the mother, and it is rarely necessary. Most of the time, the delivery of the placenta happens without interference from us of any kind.

We are extremely flexible about when we cut the cord. As long as mother and baby are happy together, there is no reason to do so if it is long enough to allow easy contact between mother and baby. When we do sever it before the delivery of the placenta, we do not always find it necessary to use clamps. We can just as well tie a knot in the cord on the baby's side. In any case, we never clamp the side nearest the mother, for that seems to inhibit the detachment of the placenta.

A mother from England

I was lifted from behind again for the final contraction and the baby was born with, I think, two pushes. She seemed to slither out by her own weight. In the birthing room I never once considered special breathing, panting, or pushing—I just did what I felt right to get the baby born. I was lowered to a sitting position as the baby appeared. Dr. Odent gathered the baby up and handed it to me immediately with the words

"There is your baby." I shall never forget those four words as long as I live. I was left to hold the baby and get to know it. The first feeling was a need to hold, the second was curiosity as to sex; she was a little girl, and I can quite clearly remember this discovery feeling like a privilege rather than a right, because the doctors had not allowed it at my two previous births. I repeated the word hello—revelling in greeting her at last. The others simply watched. No one interrupted. No one attempted to take her away.

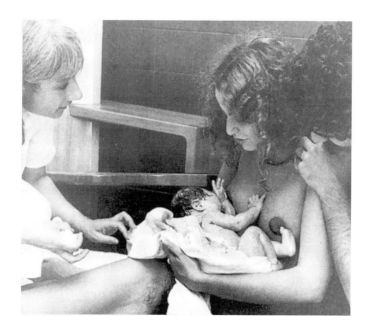

A mother from the United States

As I walked into the birthing room, I felt another contraction start. I squatted and leaned against the bed. The waters broke as I pushed with that contraction, and my three-year-old daughter Alyssa, startled, gave a little cry; she had not expected that. Dr. Odent spoke softly to her in English, explaining that the baby would be here very soon. I pushed and the baby's head crowned. I rested; then, with the next contraction, I pushed again. Finally, a third time. It felt like riding the summer waves at the shore in New Jersey during my high-school years—the breakers were very high and the highest always seemed to come in threes. All the while Dr. Odent continued to speak gently to Alyssa, reassuring her—yes, indeed it is the baby's head—see the hair—here she comes.

With that contraction, Genevieve was born. They laid her on the floor, then helped me to a sitting position. I picked her up and she began to nuzzle immediately at my breast. After a few minutes, they brought in a little tub and I bathed her there between my legs—the cord still attached. Alyssa and George helped, too. Then the cord was clamped and George cut it. The midwife took her out of the water and weighed her, dressed her, and gave her to Alyssa to hold. Alyssa was ecstatic—she had wanted a baby sister. When Genevieve started to fuss, Alyssa said, "Mama, you'd better nurse her." About thirty minutes after the birth, George held Genevieve and the nurses supported me while I squatted and delivered the placenta.

A mother from Dijon

Two forceful pushes, and Amelie entered the world. She shot out like a cannonball, landing in a graceful arc on the warm sheets held by the midwife. She came out so quickly that for a fraction of a second I thought she had landed on the floor. It was one-fifteen in the morning. The midwife placed her on my stomach. I sat down exhausted amidst my own warm blood. The athletic feat I had just accomplished had completely drained me.

I kept repeating the same words: "Is this mine? Is this really mine?" "Amelie, it's over now, we made it!" I began to explore my baby, this minuscule being who was kicking about without making a sound. First I noticed that it was a girl. I was delighted; I had been hoping for a girl all along. Then I took a closer look at her face. Her fine, clear features bore the faint tracings of a smile. She was small and so pretty. We just couldn't stop looking at her.

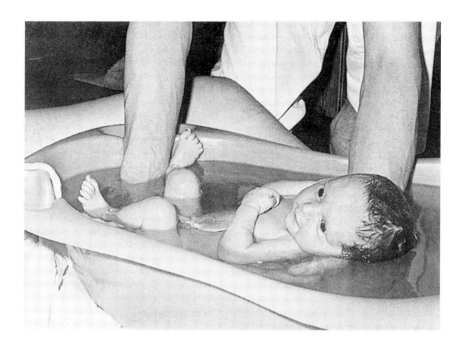

Sometimes—either before or after the placenta is expelled—we place a small basin filled with lukewarm water near the mother so that she can bathe her baby. This is not, however, routine; newborns first need their mothers' arms.

People sometimes ask us why we bathe babies so soon after birth. We can't really answer that question: it's as though they were asking, "Why pleasure?" Anyone who has ever seen a newborn lying in the bath, eyes wide open, happy to discover the world, doesn't ask such questions. Of course, bathing does have a physiological benefit as well: it is an excellent and agreeable way to stimulate the baby's skin.

The technique of giving a bath is not most important; the practiced hands of a professional may know better how to support the baby's neck and not its head, how confidently to immerse its neck and ears, but the hands of parents are certainly preferable.

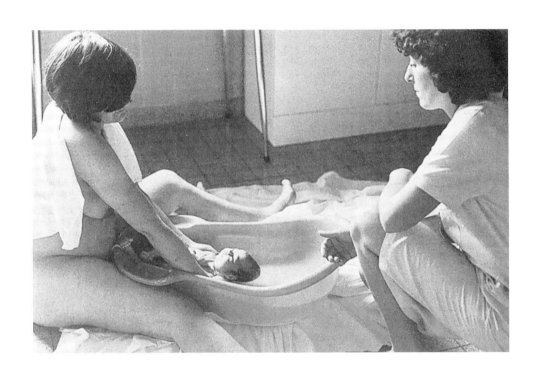

Moreover, our emphasis on the mother's bathing the newborn calls into question an assumption common in traditional obstetrics —that the woman who gives birth is passive. We can detect it even in Leboyer's practice, where the mother gives birth lying on her back and it is the doctor, midwife, or father who bathes the baby. Thus the bath becomes part of the separation of mother and child: it is intended to compensate the baby for the shock of this separation by enabling it to return to the watery warmth and gentleness of the months in the mother's womb. For us, the bath has a very different meaning: it is something the mother does herself as part of her continuing close contact with her child. I became aware of this difference at a conference where Leboyer's film *Birth* was shown after a film of a mother bathing her baby at Pithiviers. The audience reacted negatively to Leboyer's bathing scene, perceiving in it the elimination of the mother. Perhaps if the films had been shown in correct chronological order (Leboyer's coming first), the audience would have seen that we have simply taken his positive ideas a step further.

In fact, Leboyer's work has, overall, made us much more sensitive to how we handle newborns. After bathing the baby and cutting the cord, for instance, we weigh the infant, but never measure it at this time; as Leboyer points out, measurement involves a painful and unnecessary stretching of the baby's spine, and in any case results only in a very approximate number. After the weighing, we dress the infant.

The mother now takes her child back into her arms, and eventually the newborn begins to suckle again, or for the first time. The time of first suckling varies with every mother and child. It may happen right away or not until a half hour or an hour after birth. Usually the "rooting reflex" appears within an hour, and we watch as the baby turns its head from side to side to find its mother's nipple.

For early suckling to take place in the birthing room, we must create conditions that stimulate the baby's senses to function fully. It is easiest for the infant to nurse when the mother sits up straight rather than reclines backward, because her nipple is then most accessible to the baby's mouth. And it is best if the baby's hands can move around unencumbered. Some time ago we began to swathe newborns in receiving blankets, since dressing them after the bath meant keeping them from their mothers for a longer time.

Soon, however, we noticed that these babies generally began to suckle later, and we understood that this was related to the fact that their hands were not free to touch their mothers' skin.

All the senses play a role in early attachment. Infants probably establish their first links to their mothers partly on the basis of smell; hence hospital antiseptic odors can have an intrusive effect on early attachment. So can the presence of many people at the birth. Quiet is all-important. The fewer the people, the less noise, and the easier it is for a mother and child to communicate with each other. Since babies open their eyes as they suck, the room should be dimly lit, so as not to startle them. It's worth remarking that the basic needs of the woman in labor— dim lighting, quiet, and warmth—are the same as those of the newborn.

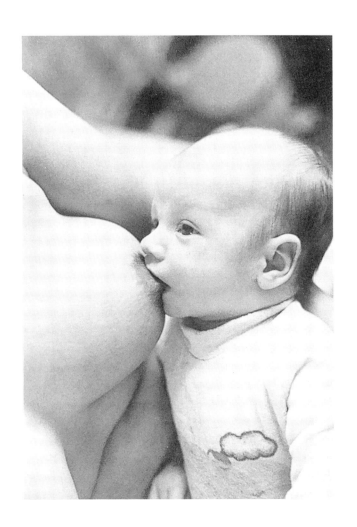

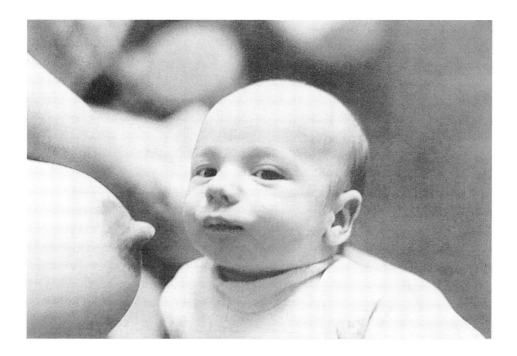

Though we have watched this scene thousands of times, we still look on with endless wonder. Not only do infants know how to look for and find their mothers' breasts almost immediately, but mothers also know just what to do—they act instinctively to help their babies nurse. A mother will sit up, pull her child close to her breast, look into its eyes, and move the breast around until the nipple is in the baby's mouth. Sometimes even a mother who had no intention whatever of breastfeeding will start to nurse her baby right after birth, not remembering until some hours later that she had planned to bottle-feed.

The sequence of events is only slightly different when babies are born in the water—a special event at Pithiviers. It is very moving to watch a child float up to the water's surface. I remember one baby who came out all by herself without any assistance. The cord was very long, and we actually saw the child swim up to the surface! In the case of water births the room should not be overheated, because contact with cool air is especially effective in stimulating the baby's first breaths as it is lifted out of the pool. To this day, we have never needed to clear breathing passages after such a birth, nor have we had even minor infections or complications associated with underwater births. Usually, after a water birth, the mother will kneel and welcome her child into the world just as she would if she were out of the pool. If the baby feels cold, nothing is easier than a warm bath then and there. But we have never attempted to prolong an infant's immersion after birth, as some do. The newborn needs human warmth, needs to be in its mother's arms and feel her gentle touch. And although some women wish to linger in the pool after giving birth, we prefer that they leave the water just before expelling the placenta, to eliminate any possibility of water entering the bloodstream via the open blood vessels in the uterus and causing an embolism.

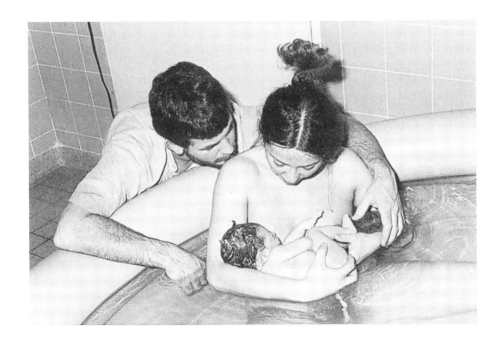

The first hour after birth has only recently become a subject of scientific study. Until the 1930s and 1940s, psychoanalysts were really the only ones to recognize the importance of early childhood. Their interest in infancy, however, remained academic and abstract. They spent little, if any, time with mothers and newborns. They focused on the maternal symbolism of milk and breasts, and overemphasized the importance of hunger-satisfaction in the formation of the mother-child bond. Their exclusive concentration on this connection obscured the fact that an infant has other needs—for example, the need for contact. This received emphasis in the work of Konrad Lorenz and Nikolaas Tinbergen published in the early 1950s, which brought ethology—the scientific study of animal behavior—into the public eye for the first time. Everyone then heard about Lorenz's goslings, which attached themselves after birth to the first large body they came in contact with, believing even a bearded man or a cardboard goose to be their mother.

With ethology came the concepts of "attachment," "bonding," and "critical" or "sensitive" periods—the relatively brief phases during which major behavioral changes are thought to occur. Scientists began to study early mother-child relations in birds, rats, goats, and apes. But to this day, hardly any ethological studies have investigated early ties between human mothers and their babies. The few that have tried are difficult to interpret, because of the uncon-

trolled interference of medical personnel and technology into the birth process common in Western hospitals.

Research during the 1960s provided evidence of the physiological, specifically hormonal, bases of this attachment.[4] In 1968, Terkel and Rosenblatt attempted to determine whether or not certain substances regulating maternal behavior were carried in blood plasma. They injected one group of virgin rats with blood plasma taken from mother rats within twenty-four hours of delivery, and another group of virgin rats with plasma from rats that had not delivered. Still another group was injected with a saline solution. The virgin rats injected with plasma from maternal rats showed maternal behavior significantly earlier than the rats in other groups. The onset of maternal behavior, therefore, seemed connected with the activity of sexual hormones—the raised levels of estrogen and prolactin and lowered levels of progesterone in the blood of rats immediately after delivery. Injections of such hormones confirmed this finding. Still, a great deal of data remained unexplained. For example, rats not injected with post-delivery plasma from other rats exhibited the same maternal behavior after continuous exposure to baby rats for several days. This was true even of males! Eventually, Terkel and Rosenblatt were led to posit a "transition period" during which regulation of maternal behavior shifted from a hormonal to a nonhormonal basis.

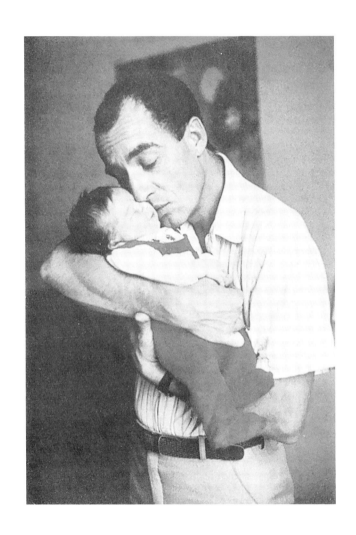

Suddenly, in the last decade, the discovery of neurohormones provided another important clue to the physiological basis of "bonding."[5] We do not yet know precisely how the neurohormonal system works, but we do know that endorphins, the neurohormones that relieve pain, also stimulate feelings of pleasure and well-being; that they come into play in friendship, love, sex, and affective relationships of all kinds, where they induce care-giving "grooming" behavior and produce habits of mutual dependence. Neurohormones, then, play a role in all forms of attachment and affection in daily life, independent of the activity of the sexual hormones. They may eventually explain the activation of maternal behavior even in the absence of parturition.

Neurohormones also figure importantly during childbirth, both during labor (when, as we have seen, they help to relieve pain) and after delivery. When we note that endorphin levels are elevated in maternal and infant blood following birth, we see how the endorphin system contributes to creating an interdependency between mother and child —the bonding process. The fact that the maternal blood level of endorphins is higher following vaginal birth than cesarean section is yet another argument against disturbing the birth process. A similar criticism applies to the use of painkillers and synthetic hormones, which, by competing with natural hormones, alter the complex natural hormonal balance, affect how the mother feels after birth, and thus influence the dynamics of bonding.

All these findings encourage us to attend carefully to and facilitate this first, important contact between mother and child. The baby's initial bond with another human being could serve as a wonderful model of what attachment and affection can be like. This is not to say that mothers and babies who do not have the opportunity for such ideal first contact are worse off in the long run than those who do, or that these infants will necessarily be less rooted as adults, less able to love or to feel pleasure. Culture, environment, and social conditioning will have a greater effect on any individual than what happens during a few early "critical" periods, and can certainly compensate for anything lacking at the start. Human beings,

after all, are not goslings. But why not make the start as positive as possible? Why not increase everybody's chances? Are we obstetricians and midwives not, as professionals, responsible for something beyond strictly medical assistance? Altering the initial contacts people have with others at the start of their lives is one concrete way we can act to humanize our world.

At Pithiviers, after the delivery of the placenta, the mother, child, father, midwife, and occasionally the doctor, move into a warm bedroom close by. By this time the baby has usually started suckling. The mother will often walk to her room holding her child in her arms. In each of these rooms, beside the bed there is a wooden cradle,

In the bedroom

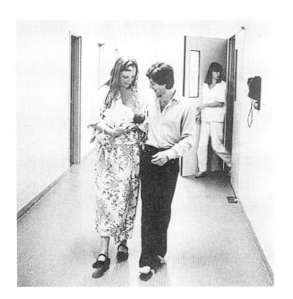

handcrafted by the father of a baby born at Pithiviers. In addition, there is a very low chair, an actual *"prie-dieu"* (prayer stool), which seems to have been specially designed for the ease and comfort of the nursing mother. Women are free to have any guests they like. An extra bed is always available for the person accompanying the mother.

There is, of course, no central nursery at Pithiviers. Babies always stay with their mothers. The same midwives who helped the mother during labor are also at hand during the mother's postpartum stay at the hospital. They are assisted by a number of women, most of whom are themselves mothers. These assistants, several of whom have worked here for over twenty years, tidy up the rooms and serve meals. They also show

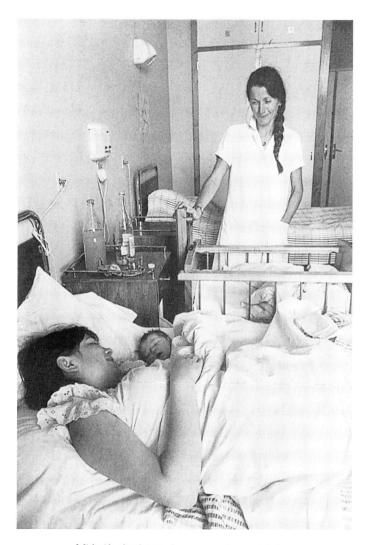

Midwife checks on sleeping mother and baby

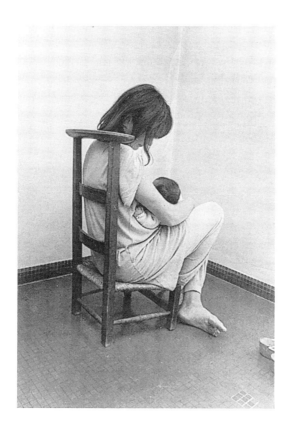

new mothers how to change diapers, offer helpful advice on breastfeeding, and report any unusual circumstances—like jaundice or changes in the baby's behavior—to one of the midwives or the doctor. The work of the midwives and assistants frees a mother of all material concerns during her stay at the clinic, so that she is able to focus on her child and herself. No hospital rules or routines interfere with the growing relationship between mother and child.

In such an environment, it is easily possible to satisfy the basic needs of a newborn. Babies need the soothing presence of the mother: her warmth, her touch, her voice, her smell, the feel of her skin. Babies need to move around, to be rocked in their mothers' arms. Rocking a baby has been underrated since the turn of the century; pediatricians, preoccupied with germs and calories, have given little thought to vestibular function, which regulates balance and other motor co-

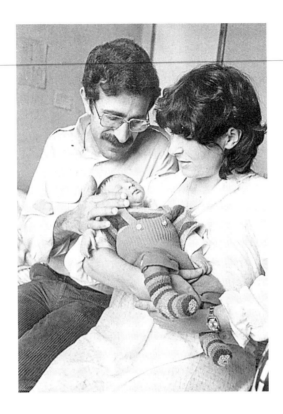

ordination and which requires stimulation—
in this case, provided by rocking—for its development. Naturally, babies also need to
nurse, and especially to nurse when they
please.

These fundamental needs are most readily
satisfied when a mother stays as close to her
newborn as possible, both day and night. Babies seem calmer and happier in their mothers' beds than in their cradles, even when the
mother is not around, perhaps because there
they can still perceive and be comforted by

her scent. Mothers are encouraged to change
their babies themselves and to give them
daily baths, the latter a unique aspect of life
at Pithiviers. At one time there was a hospital
policy against bathing a child until after the
umbilical cord fell off, which usually meant
about a two-week wait. Since 1963, however,
mothers at our unit have been bathing their
babies from birth onward without any problems—and to the great pleasure of both.
With respect to nutrition, a mother who stays
with her child around the clock will quickly

learn its needs and desires. She will develop a sensitivity to her baby's expressions, and won't interpret every cry as a demand for milk, which so often leads to breastfeeding problems.

We encourage patience in the establishment of breastfeeding. In order to diminish any pressures a new mother might feel, we remind her that babies don't really need milk or many calories until they are two or three days old. In fact, before this time the breasts don't actually contain milk but rather colostrum, a high-quality fluid rich in antibodies. It isn't until about the third day that milk, as such, is actually let down. Sometimes there are timing problems: either the milk may come in before the baby first develops an appetite, or the baby may get hungry before there is milk. The assistants can really help at times like these to reassure the mother and keep her from feeling impatient or frustrated. The possibility of such problems makes the third day after birth the worst one for leaving the clinic. Women are certainly not required to stay at the clinic for any specific length of time, and are free to go home whenever they want. Most, however, find that the best time to leave is either within the first two days after birth or not until four or five days later.

Momentary frustrations aside, postpartum depression is rare in our clinic. Many people who have worked or given birth in large hospitals are quick to notice how relatively few women at Pithiviers get depressed after birth. It is plausible that the way women give birth at Pithiviers itself makes them less vulnerable to depression. We know that postpartum "blues" are, to some extent, the result of hormonal imbalances. Every birth is followed by sudden alterations in the levels of estrogen, progesterone, prolactin, oxytocin, and endorphins. By respecting a woman's hormonal balance during labor and birth, however, and by avoiding the use of drugs, we probably eliminate many abnormal hormonal fluctuations and thereby decrease the likelihood of postpartum depression. Moreover, the supportive environment at the clinic may well have a consoling and nurturant effect on vulnerable, new mothers. Still another factor may well be that mothers at our clinic take such an active part in caring for their children, which both creates a sense of fulfillment and familiarizes a first-time mother with her new responsibilities. Thus, when a woman leaves us to go

home, she is not suddenly faced with an entirely new and frustrating situation, but instead is already used to and comfortable with caring for her child.

Outside of clinics like our own, there are very few places devoted to meeting a newborn's needs. For instance, the infant's need to be able to identify its mother and have her close is often impossible to satisfy in the majority of modern hospital environments. Members of the hospital staff frequently take the place of the mother, and cause needless confusion for the child. Nurseries in China and Eastern Europe are almost caricatures of this situation: dozens of babies lie tightly wrapped, lined up side by side, to be carried like packages to their mothers at feeding time. One glance at such scenes makes one acutely aware of the need for change. Ironically, at Pithiviers the strongest resistance to change is often from the mothers of the women who come to us to give birth. This is particularly true if they gave birth in the 1950s and 1960s, at a time when breastfeeding was not valued and women were told again and again that excessive attention would "spoil" a child, that feeding on demand would lead to the development of "bad habits." These women are uncomfortable when they see their daughters or daughters-in-law respond to their babies' needs to be fed, held, and cuddled on demand.

Obviously, if a mother will not "listen" to her baby for fear of encouraging "bad habits," the child will have no choice in the end but to submit to such treatment. But sooner or later there will be a price to pay. Though not entirely conclusive, results of a number of important studies show correlations between certain events during fetal life, childbirth, and infancy and a variety of later illnesses. For example, Nikolaas Tinbergen, the British ethologist and Nobel Prize winner, has identified specific factors such as rough forceps delivery and prolonged separation from the mother after birth as "pathogenic" (disease-producing); in this case, as possible causes of autism.

Personally, I had always been predisposed to give great weight to the importance of early childhood and infancy because of my mother's work as a nursery school teacher. She was deeply influenced by such figures as Maria Montessori, a pioneer of early childhood education who studied the possible long-term effects of a baby's experiences during the first hours of its life on its later development. Montessori's work took on new meaning for me at the stage of my life when, at Pithiviers, my earlier medical experience converged with our reconsideration of obstetrical practice. As a surgeon, I often treated adults for diseases like peptic ulcer, ulcerative colitis, and hyperthyroidism. Each time I sought to discover the origin and nature of these so-called "psychosomatic" illnesses, I was inevitably led back to a consideration of the patient's early childhood. Treating such illnesses and working at the maternity unit at the same time focused my continuing interest in infancy and the beginnings of the mother-child relationship. I became curious about the psychoanalytic perspective and intrigued with the work of ethologists who had studied the first contacts between animal mothers and their offspring and investigated the critical periods of the bonding process.

The fascinating concept of "inhibition of action," formulated by Henri Laborit—the French physiologist who in 1952 introduced chlorpromazine, the first neuroleptic (behavior-modifying) drug—provides an important key to our understanding of the connection between early traumas and later development. Laborit used the term "inhibition of action" to describe the basic submissive behavioral pattern, a pathogenic state, that results when an organism is unable to respond to stress by either fighting or fleeing. In experiments with rats, Laborit was able to trace the origin of high blood pressure to just such situations of continuous frustration. Rats in a cage received repeated electric shocks. Some had access to an open door; others could not flee. Some were in a cage with other rats and could fight; others were isolated. Only those rats who could neither fight nor flee suffered a definitive rise in blood pressure. The point is that the exact nature or cause of stress is a less significant factor than how or whether one can act to relieve it. This is certainly true

in humans. We need only think of how upsetting such situations of frustration without possibility of relief or resolution are in our own lives.

Hormonal studies confirm Laborit's theories. "Inhibition of action" generates the secretion of noradrenaline and cortisol; cortisol itself triggers the inhibition of action—the result being a vicious circle that accounts for the genesis of anguish. Only an action that violates the pattern by bringing a reward can break the cycle. Moreover, since we know that noradrenaline contracts the blood vessels, quickens the heartbeat, and raises blood pressure, and that cortisol has many kinds of long-term effects, such as depressing the immune system and destroying the thymus, we can predict dire consequences in cases of repeated inhibition of action. It is obvious that such continued hormonal reactions to pathogenic situations are factors (along with genetic and other causes) in the etiology of what we used to call "psychosomatic diseases." These include depression, high blood pressure, ulcers, allergies, sexual dysfunction, difficult deliveries, colitis, irregularities of the immune system, cancer—in short, all the maladies we associate with modern civilization.

Although Laborit does not explicitly relate his findings to the common experiences of newborns, he might well have done so. It is precisely in the very early phases of life, when the "hormonostat" in the brain that regulates the body's hormonal level is set, that these behavioral situations are most likely to give rise to pathology.[6] Many infants spend days, weeks, and even months in prolonged, almost chronic states of "inhibition of action." Separated from their mothers for hours at a time, subjected to rough medical examinations, their demands for food ignored, they probably learn quite early on that their crying will have little or no effect on what goes on around them. Indeed, our mothers and grandmothers were taught that babies must not be "spoiled"—in other words, that they must be kept in a state of "inhibition of action." At Pithiviers, our aim is to prevent these pathogenic situations by satisfying the fundamental needs of the baby. The best way is to insure that, in the early days, mother and child are together and accessible to each other at all times.

If conventional hospitals rarely satisfy the fundamental needs of full-term infants, the situation is even more acute in the case of premature babies. Nowadays, prematurity is viewed as a handicap and feared because it is so often associated with greater susceptibility to disease, emotional problems, and mental retardation. Yet, without denying the potential problems of prematurity, let us remember that Galileo, Pascal, Darwin, and Einstein were all born prematurely—and in a sense, all human beings, compared to most other mammals, are born at a stage of imma-turity (their systems not yet fully formed). Their maturation occurs within a social context, where they experience early, intense sensory stimulation. The specific kinds of stimulation vary from one culture to another, and one individual to another, but sensory stimulation of some kind is universal. What can this tell us about infants born "before term?" Although the maturation of the central nervous system is determined by certain chronological imperatives linked to the genetic code, the awakening of sensory functions is clearly an essential stimulus to its development. For example, simple tests have shown that infants at forty-five weeks from conception who were born prematurely usually have more advanced vestibular function than infants of the same age born at term. Prematurity does not, then, necessarily lead to physical and emotional incapacity; on the contrary, premature babies promptly exposed to rich and varied stimulation may well become some of the most advanced in their development. Perhaps some of our prematurely born geniuses were exposed to exceptionally rich sensory experiences at a very early age—a likely hypothesis because, in the days prior to the existence of neonatology, premature babies probably owed their survival to the constant sensitivity and vigilance of attentive and responsive mothers.

Today, prematurity is unfortunately characterized by mother-child separation and acute sensory deprivation at a crucial devel-

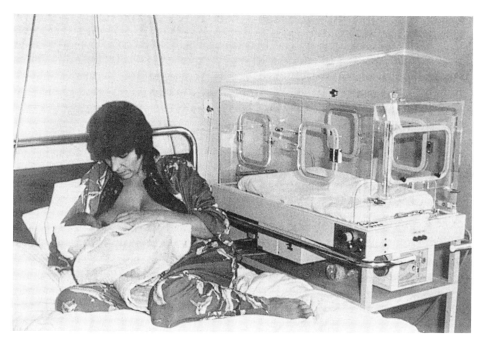

Mother keeps premature baby in her bed,
with incubator alongside

opmental period in the baby's life. A premature infant in an intensive care nursery often receives *less* kinesthetic and vibratory stimulation than a fetus of the same age *in utero*—when, in fact, it needs more. The environment in that humid glass or plastic cage called an incubator is obviously isolating, and the constant noise of the motor serves to mask all the sounds that may have any meaning for the baby. The child can neither touch its mother nor hear her voice. This is disheartening in light of the special importance of sensory stimuli and human contact to such a child. Food and warmth will not suffice to bring energy to the brain, or to exercise early motor functions.

For a start, why not simply take the incubator out of the intensive care unit and put it into the mother's room? Every mother can understand that an incubator is merely a glass or plastic box with a built-in thermostat, quite a manageable piece of technology. Furthermore, putting an extra heater in the room makes it possible to take the baby out of the incubator without risk. Swathed in warm blankets, even the premature baby can spend most of its time in the mother's arms being rocked, touched, caressed, tickled, spoken to, or nursed. The premature infant, too, can get to know its mother, become used to her voice, her scent, and her touch. In fact, the composition of its mother's milk is perfectly adapted to the special needs of the premature infant.[7] Not surprisingly, most mothers at Pithiviers choose to use the incubators as little as possible, preferring to keep their babies in bed with them. When a premature baby and its mother are together all the time, it is quite astonishing how quickly they become an autonomous unit, independent of the hospital personnel. Given this intimate contact, the mother will know her baby best: if something unusual happens, she will always be the first to notice.

The smallest babies we have kept at the clinic and not sent to a neonatal intensive care unit were a pair of twins, each weighing 3.7 pounds. During their stay at Pithiviers, the twins were separated from their mother only once—for an hour, when she went to run some errands in town. We have never had to send babies under 5.5 pounds to the pediatrics unit after deciding to care for them at the clinic. What is more, we were consistently impressed by the rapid progress these children made in their mothers' care and often agreed to let them be taken home while they were still underweight. (By contrast, such babies in neonatal care units would be

kept in incubators for an additional week or two.) Indeed, we have come to suspect that many of the metabolic disturbances frequently observed in premature infants are linked not to prematurity itself, but rather to the absence or reduction of sensory stimulation and human affection—specifically to the separation of mother and child—common in most modern hospitals.

Unfortunately, practical obstacles often make this ideal closeness between mother and child impossible, even in our unit. A mother who already has several children at home is sometimes unable to stay in the hospital for several weeks with her baby. Moreover, the French national insurance is not easily persuaded to cover the cost of her hospitalization for longer than twelve days, even though it is usually less expensive than a newborn's stay in an intensive care unit. These practical difficulties are, to an extent, also linked to our perhaps excessive prudence. Despite the harshness of incubators, we are not yet ready simply to dispense with them altogether. And we do not yet feel ready to follow the example of Edgar Rey, the Colombian pediatrician who sends premature babies home after only one or two days, advising the mothers to stay with them day and night in close body contact. But perhaps one day. . . .

The results of our approach to prematurity are not yet statistically interpretable; we simply haven't had enough cases to date. Even so, our approach finds support in the fact that, of the forty-eight premature babies born over the past four years at Pithiviers, each weighing less than 5.5 pounds, not one has had to be hospitalized subsequently.

Before a mother leaves the maternity unit, we talk with her about a variety of subjects, from contraception to baby carriers. We make sure to tell her about La Leche League, the international organization founded twenty-five years ago by women who wanted to make breastfeeding easier and more reward-

ing for both mothers and babies. It is important that women be informed about what to expect when breastfeeding, since many doctors know so little about it that they can't advise mothers what to do when problems arise, and all too quickly counsel them to quit.

At this point, we let the mother take over from the hospital. We remain available to help, should she have any problems. But if we have done our job properly, she will now be ready and eager to manage on her own.

It was spring. Every Tuesday we went to sing with Marie-Louise at the maternity unit. I was two months pregnant when we made our first visit. As school let out, I could hear my five-year-old daughter boasting to her friends: "I'm going to dance and sing at the hospital where babies are born."

Fantasy: Marie-Louise sings of life and my child sings of life inside me. Summer comes to Pithiviers, flooding the town with sunlight. Golden fields cover the earth of Beauce. We spend our vacation at the country inn run by Madame de la Forge. She works at the hospital and sings there, too. Her hospitality knows no bounds.

During an appointment one day with a pediatrician, my daughter is drawn towards Martine, a young mother-to-be. They play together and make paper birds. A friendship is born. Okay, I promise, tomorrow we'll all have a picnic together on the grass. But the next day, Martine and Didier, our new friends, are not there to meet us. At the hospital, an attendant informs us that their child is about to be born in Room 126. We go for a short visit. Didier asks me to stay with Martine for five minutes or so while he has a cigarette. They were out camping when the first "signs" began during the night.

Martine is about to give birth. She wants to share this with me, to bring back the ancient bonds between women. Martine sits in the pool to ease the powerful contractions. My daughter tiptoes in and out. Should I try to keep her away from the reality of birth? Soon I hear her playing the piano down the hall in the singing room; her little hands touch the keys like butterfly wings brushing each other in a grassy field. The baby's head has crowned. "I've run out of strength, I . . . ." Martine moans.

Martine's child is born, and cries gently in her arms. "My son," she says with amazement, "you have your own life now!" The sweat on my face is mixed with tears of joy. "Can we go have our picnic now?" chirps my daughter, as she comes into the room.

Several days later, she asks thoughtfully, "Mommy, is that what life is?" "Yes," I answer. Her reply: "Oh, it's great!"

A month later, we are making the familiar trip from Paris to Pithiviers. The villagers are celebrating a local holiday. Flowers. Fanfares. Majorettes. My contractions, which began that morning, become regular as we follow in step with the music.

At about eight in the evening, I unpack my suitcase in Room 126. My husband enchants our daughter with magical witch stories. She soon falls asleep.

At the stroke of midnight, Baptiste is born.

His father supported me with all his strength, an attendant making sure his precious grip was firm. Our midwife waited patiently. There I was, sitting on the floor, my baby in my arms. A small bath was prepared for him. A student nurse whom I'd met at the singing sessions sat at my back, supporting me comfortably. I watched as Baptiste's father cut the umbilical cord, which was still attached within me.

We returned to our room, Baptiste in his father's arms. In bed, Baptiste lies asleep beside me. He wakes up, tries to nurse, goes back to sleep again. I remember another night of birth, a sleepless night, gray with sadness, an emptiness surrounding me: as soon as my daughter was born, she was taken away, so that I could rest! Here at Pithiviers, they don't take your children away from you. New bonds are given time and space to grow.

The next day, a nurse suggests that we change little Baptiste. But he is sleeping. So we wait. And I am still there when he wakes up. They simply give me general advice: I know what to do.

Four months have passed. The knot so solidly tied at Pithiviers has become stronger with each day. Look at Baptiste, leaving my breast to smile at me, to look at his father, whose voice he hears! The first time he did this, he didn't realize that by smiling he would lose my nipple, and he began to howl. When he found it again, he smiled once more!

At Pithiviers, I was alive throughout birth, able to cherish every moment. I shared my experience with women attendants infinitely attentive to me and my child. And for a man, it must be an unforgettable experience to help the woman he loves give birth.

I dry off shivering Baptiste after his bath, and sing to him the tender words of Marie-Louise:

Tu n'auras jamais froid,
Je sèmerai la laine,
Tu n'auras jamais froid,
Je planterai la soie . . . .

You'll never be cold,
I'll sow seeds of wool,
You'll never be cold,
I'll plant silks untold . . . .

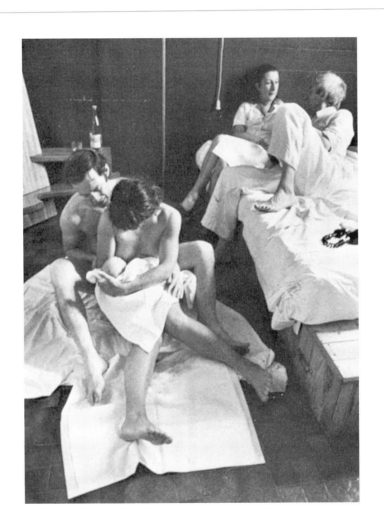

anti-obstetrics

It is easy to imagine a conventional obstetrician's objections to our way of handling birth at Pithiviers. Such a doctor might argue that our practice is suitable only for healthy women with "low-risk" pregnancies (who are expected to deliver without complications) and that for all other women, it is potentially dangerous. It is true that most births at Pithiviers are unproblematic. This is not, however, due to a particularly low-risk population at the clinic. We do not screen prospective mothers and send those with possible problems to another hospital. Nor do we advertise to attract only a certain segment of the population. In fact, many women who come to Pithiviers are there precisely because they have experienced trouble with previous labors and births. Some, having been to many other doctors and maternity units, are extremely upset and worried, and because of this, we cannot expect an easy labor or delivery. Others have been considered special or difficult cases elsewhere and want to know what we can do differently for them. For instance, it is typical at our clinic to find women in their late thirties or early forties who have already had cesarean sections and now want a chance to have a natural labor and to deliver vaginally if possible. In addition, a maternity clinic about fifteen miles away still has no surgical facilities and sends us women who develop problems in the course of labor. Certainly these women do not qualify as low-risk pregnancies.

We have, then, at least our fair share of difficult cases. Yet for nine out of ten women who give birth at Pithiviers, warmth, calm, quiet, freedom of movement, and the presence of sensitive birth attendants are sufficient to insure a smooth progression of labor. Indeed, the harder we expect a labor to be, the more we pay attention to the *quality* of the atmosphere. Problems are the exception, even with those women whose past experiences would lead us to believe otherwise.

The medical establishment repeatedly cites the "risk factor"—the legitimate concern for the safety of mother and child—to justify the wholesale "medicalization" of the birth process and to discredit all alternatives, whether home births, birthing centers outside the hospital, or in-hospital maternity units such as Pithiviers. But it is not at all clear that this approach—which involves the widespread use of sedatives, artificial hormones to stimulate labor, epidurals and other anesthesia, forceps, and the daily performance of cesareans—has lowered the "risk factor," since much of this medical intervention actually in-

troduces new risks. Moreover, this emphasis on high-risk cases poorly serves the interests of the vast majority of women, who have "normal" pregnancies and deliveries. Unfortunately, most doctors are far more interested in sickness than in health. They assume that good health is merely the absence of illness. As a result, doctors and medical students frequently address obstetrics only as it pertains to pathology. They spend most of their time preparing for all the awful things that could go wrong during pregnancy and childbirth. Students learn all about placenta previa and acute toxemia, but by the time they are doctors, they have learned little about the physiology of normal labor and are ignorant of the perfectly common factors which might modify the process without being cause for alarm or intervention. The end result is that birth itself, every birth, is seen as a potential problem.

At Pithiviers, of course, we do not hesitate to intervene medically when necessary. We are not opposed to medical technology, and we do not deny the importance of technological contributions to the field of obstetrics. We certainly steer clear of any unnecessary risk to mother and baby. Our dedication to helping women give birth on their own, however, determines when and how we intervene, should a problem arise; because every woman's situation is different, there cannot be a standardized or routine pattern of intervention. And because we consider birth a personal, intimate event, we make every effort to lessen the invasive nature of medical assistance. As it turns out, many aspects of our practice eliminate the very dangers that conventional obstetrics has created: when women have the freedom to move around during labor and to assume vertical birthing positions, certain complications never arise and many commonplace interventions become unnecessary.

Take, for example, the artificial rupture of the membranes, a procedure that has become increasingly common, although its medical justification is debatable. In modern hospitals, it is common early in labor to break the membranes enclosing the waters in which the fetus floats. When the pressure of a contraction causes the membranes to bulge, they can be broken easily with any blunt instrument. One reason doctors give for this procedure (amniotomy) is that it accelerates labor, which is assumed to be desirable. Another reason many practitioners break the membranes is to determine the color of the amniotic fluid. This color can be a helpful clue to the baby's condition and may sometimes indicate fetal distress. If a fetus is deprived of oxygen at any time, it will protect its vital organs, such as the heart and brain, and compromise oxygen flow to other, less crucial organs. When this happens, the intestines retract and empty themselves into the amniotic fluid, giving it a yellow, green, or brownish tinge that suggests the baby has suffered or is suffering oxygen deprivation. A third reason for breaking the waters is to

enable doctors to use an electric internal fetal monitor, which requires clipping an electrode onto the baby's scalp to check for fetal distress.

From our point of view, none of these is a good enough reason for routine intervention. First of all, it is not at all clear why routine acceleration of labor is desirable. For one thing, breaking the waters makes infection more likely for both mother and infant. This is especially so if a woman must endure labor on her back, because in this position the fluid cannot run down and out. Breaking the membranes also destroys their potential function as extra protection for the cord and the baby's skull during the final stages of labor. Finally, in those cases where breaking the membranes seems to accelerate labor, it probably means the membranes would have broken soon on their own.

At Pithiviers, in order to let labor take its natural physiological course, we rarely break the waters. Instead, if we think it necessary to do a special check on the baby's condition, we inspect the membranes with an amnioscope: a metal tube equipped with a light at one end. With the amnioscope we can see the color of the amniotic fluid through the transparent membranes, without having to break them. Nor do we find much reason to use internal electronic monitoring to check and record the fetal heartbeat continuously. For one thing, this aggressive intrusion on the baby's world is not without risk. For another, it is primarily when a woman is immobilized on her back, with the uterus pressing against the vena cava and her contractions augmented by synthetic hormones, that the baby is likely to suffer—which is when constant electronic monitoring becomes necessary. At our clinic, where women move around freely and drugs are not used, the two principal causes of fetal distress are eliminated. It is thus unnecessary for us to do more than listen intermittently to the fetal heartbeat with a conventional obstetrical stethoscope. If the woman is standing or if she is in the pool, it is more practical to use the Doptone, a small instrument that looks like an electric razor and uses a very low-frequency ultrasound wave to detect the baby's heart movements. The Doptone is considered safe by many physicians because its wave is low in pressure and intensity; nevertheless, because its long-term effects are not yet known, we are careful not to use it earlier in pregnancy; if we have to use it during labor, we do so only for brief intervals.

There are only two situations in which we judge it necessary to break the waters. The first occurs when labor stops entirely after cervical dilation is complete—a problem we seldom encounter, since if we are patient enough, labor usually starts again spontaneously. The second is when the placenta is low but does not absolutely cover the cervical opening (marginal placenta previa). In the latter case, once the membranes are ruptured, some women are able to deliver vaginally without danger of hemorrhaging.

Aside from these special and unusual instances, however, it is not exceptional at Pithiviers for babies to be born in their "caul" (with the membranes intact, covering the head); this is a sign of good luck in many cultures around the world. Of course, sometimes the membranes break by themselves before contractions start. If this happens, we wait for labor to begin and make sure that the water is clear, an indication of the baby's health. No risk is to be anticipated from such normal, spontaneous rupture, but we refrain from performing vaginal examinations at these times in order to minimize the possibility of infection.

The routine use of Pitocin is another questionable practice. Pitocin, a synthetic form of the hormone oxytocin, is the drug used most often throughout the world during all stages of labor to stimulate or strengthen uterine contractions. Pitocin is prescribed when a woman in labor does not achieve the necessary hormonal balance or secrete enough oxytocin to generate contractions, or contractions of sufficient strength. Knowing what we do now about the effect of the environment on the woman in labor, it should come as no surprise that conventional hospital settings are not conducive to spontaneous, efficient labor. The unfamiliar surroundings, bright lights, intimidating machines, strange noises, and constant flow of strangers make it less likely that women will achieve the required hormonal equilibrium. No wonder Pitocin becomes necessary in so many hospital births. It is not an ideal alternative, however. Synthetic hormones, even in prudent doses, can never replace perfect physiological hormonal balance. Moreover, experience has taught us that contractions artificially reinforced with Pitocin are, because of their sometimes excessive strength and greater frequency, more likely to cause oxygen deprivation to the fetus than natural contractions. Finally, recent studies have shown a connection between the use of Pitocin and glucose (the sugar present in the intravenous drip solution through which Pitocin is administered) and neonatal jaundice.

At Pithiviers, therefore, we do everything possible to create an environment in which a woman will secrete her own oxytocin, making Pitocin unnecessary. We employ Pitocin in less than one birth out of a hundred, only if dilation is not progressing and the baby's descent becomes difficult. (We never administer Pitocin when babies are in breech presentations, for reasons that will be discussed later in this chapter.) We slowly begin the Pitocin drip. If the baby's heartbeat slows down even minutely, we stop the drip immediately; if all is well, we continue it until the baby has descended and dilation is complete. Sometimes even a minuscule dose is enough to bring on complete dilation and descent. As soon as possible—which means as soon as the baby has crowned and is ready to be born—we stop all Pitocin.

Opening the medication cabinet for drugs of any kind is hardly daily routine in our clinic. Except for the occasions noted above when we use Pitocin, we almost never administer drugs during labor. Narcotics, tranquilizers, and painkillers all cross the placenta and have a depressive effect on the newborn. (The long-term effects of these drugs—from Pitocin to painkillers—on the newborn are still not known; studies are in progress.) Nor do we use regional anesthesia, such as epidurals, so popular in many hospitals. An epidural is done by inserting a needle between two lumbar vertebrae, introducing a catheter, and then injecting an anesthetic that desensitizes or paralyzes the lower half of a woman's body. Epidurals lead to a lowering of blood pressure, which must then be remedied by intravenous drips, and inhibit uterine contractions, so that doses of Pitocin become necessary. When dilation is complete and the descent is finished, the woman cannot, of course, feel when to push to help the baby emerge; instead, she must be told when. If her attempts are unsuccessful, the infant must be pulled out with forceps.

Conventional obstetrics justifies the use of epidurals and other anesthetic procedures by saying that they spare mothers a great deal of pain. Epidurals do take away pain—but they also take away active participation in childbirth. Moreover, the same doctors who advocate their use refuse to recognize that much of the pain of childbirth is created by their insistence on women giving birth in a particular position; their routine use of Pitocin, which brings on unnaturally strong contractions; and their prescription of other drugs that alter the hormonal balance and probably inhibit the production of natural opiates. In a sense, conventional obstetrics leaves most women no option but to request epidurals and other artificial relief.

In our clinic, instead of resorting to drugs when a birth is particularly difficult, we encourage the prospective mother to try different positions, relax in a pool of warm water, focus inward, draw on all her resources, and rely on the support of those around her. Occasionally we suggest a drop or two of alcohol in the form of punch or champagne, to help the woman relax. We have also experimented with various alternatives to chemical painkillers. For a short time we tried acupuncture to reduce labor pain. Paradoxically, my trip to China discouraged us from pursuing this line. In fact, I learned that traditional Chinese acupuncture is rarely used in childbirth. This is not a result of ignorance or indifference on the part of male acupuncturists. On the contrary, acupuncture is used in obstetrics. The Zhiyin point on the level of the little toe is thought to turn around breech babies during pregnancy, and the Renzhong on the upper lip may be used to revive newborns. But the rarity of acupuncture in labor probably reflects a traditional attitude which wisely acknowledges that to try to influence labor means disturbing an extremely complex process that is better left untouched. Though we had some limited success with acupuncture, it was impossible to perform

while a woman was walking around, changing positions, or floating in water, so we eventually gave it up. We have only a little experience with homeopathy during pregnancy and labor, but have been surprised by the apparent efficacy of "caulophyllum 4CH" used alternatively with "actea racemosa 4CH" (pills placed under the tongue of the woman in labor). Certain midwives believe that these homeopathic remedies make labor easier, faster, and less painful.

From time to time we do perform "lumbar reflex therapy" for relief when contractions are felt painfully in the lower back and dilation has stopped at about five centimeters. This involves injecting small amounts of water intradermically in the lumbar area. Studies have shown that pain impulses originating in the skin can inhibit deep pain impulses. After an intense momentary local pain, this type of therapy usually brings immediate relief for this specific back pain and also allows dilation to progress.

Ultimately, however, when labor is especially difficult, a woman must use every strength she has to bring her child into the world. Unlike the majority of obstetricians, we trust a woman's own capacities and potential during labor, and this trust has been constantly reinforced by our experiences at the clinic.

The same is true for the moment of delivery. Obstetricians react quite strongly when we tell them that forceps have not been used at Pithiviers since 1963—and that as far as we are concerned, they belong in museums. Such passionate reactions should not be surprising, since forceps are as basic to the practice of modern obstetrics as the supine position; by eliminating both, we have, in effect, shaken the very foundations of modern obstetrical practice. One should not forget that women were first made to lie flat on their backs on high, narrow delivery tables so that doctors could use forceps more easily.

The use of forceps to remove the infant from the mother's body completely supersedes the natural process of childbirth. Anesthesia must sometimes accompany forceps deliveries, making the process all the more intrusive and dangerous. Of course, in most cases, the training and skill of the practitioner are more important than the type of instrument used. But it is unfortunately true that the forceps have yet to be designed that are safe in any hands, and there are only a few hands that can safely and gently use any forceps.

At Pithiviers, our abandonment of the dorsal position has, in fact, made forceps obsolete. In the rare cases where the mother's contractions are insufficient to push the baby out without help, even when the descent is complete and the cervix fully dilated, we use a simple device called a vacuum extractor instead. This instrument, which we employ in about 6 percent of all births at Pithiviers, consists of a small cup attached by a rubber tube to a jar. With a simple bicycle pump we can create a vacuum in the jar, causing the cup to

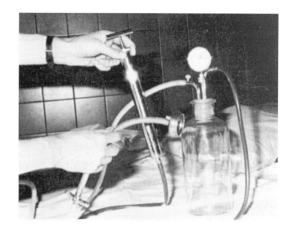

adhere to a surface. Although it can be used in any position, the vacuum extractor is usually employed with the mother in a semi-seated position supported by her partner. The cup is inserted into her vagina and placed on the baby's head, as close as possible to the mother's pubic bone. When we pump to create a vacuum, the cup adheres to the child's head. A gauge indicates the exact amount of pressure being applied. In about five minutes, the pressure reaches about 0.4 kg. per centimeter, a very low number, but sufficient for our needs. When the pressure reaches this point, we maintain a light traction on the rubber tube, pulling it gently in the direction of the baby's head. Between contractions, the cup helps to keep the infant's head from going back up into the mother's vagina. Meanwhile the mother, for her part, continues to help push the baby out, using the vacuum extractor as an aid to her own efforts. The baby's head pushing against the perineum stimulates a high secretion of oxytocin, which triggers efficient contractions (the Ferguson reflex). For this reason, if we have been using a Pitocin drip, we will discontinue it as soon as the baby has come down far enough to use a vacuum extractor. Once the contractions are good and strong, we guide the baby's head out gently but firmly with the vacuum extractor. The baby descends easily and the head usually crowns after several contractions. At this point we sometimes remove the cup and proceed as usual, while the mother takes whatever birthing position feels best. In short, the vacuum extractor is a practical, dependable instrument; it never breaks down, is extremely easy to use, and requires no anesthesia. We use it in the birthing room, but it could be used in home births as well.

After use of the vacuum extractor at the end of first-stage labor, women are usually able to use their own resources to give birth. Many mothers don't have the feeling that the baby has been extracted; some of them even forget that they were assisted by a vacuum extractor. Women whose babies have been extracted by forceps, on the other hand, never forget it. As for the babies, after vacuum extraction it is common for a small bump to appear on their heads, but this goes away completely after a few hours.

Significantly, vacuum extractors are widely known and used only in countries where women have control over the birth environment. They were originally developed in Sweden, a country with a long tradition of midwifery. In China, where most obstetricians are women, birth attendants often use a very rudimentary version of the vacuum method. Forceps, which literally take birth away from the mother and put it into the hands of the doctor, are used almost exclusively in countries where men dominate the field of obstetrics. In the United States, for example, where midwifery is not well established, the rate of forceps use is very high.

Another common procedure at the moment of delivery which we will perform only in particular circumstances is the episiotomy. An episiotomy consists of cutting the vaginal opening with scissors in order to enlarge it and so facilitate the baby's passage. It is always made at the *fourchette,* that is, at the back part of the vaginal opening. Sometimes the cut goes straight back (midline); other times, it branches to the side (mediolateral). This is usually done just before the final contractions, when the perineum is distended from the pressure of the baby's head and has become relatively insensitive; the woman feels no pain. While episiotomies are routine in most modern hospitals (95 percent), we have found them necessary in just 7 percent of all births at Pithiviers. We perform an episiotomy only when there is cause for concern about the baby's physical state—for instance, in the case of a breech presentation. An episiotomy will then spare the stressed baby those last few contractions and will enable it to be born more quickly.

The truth is that episiotomies are rarely necessary when women deliver in the supported squatting position, as is so often the case at Pithiviers. This position assures maximum pelvic pressure, optimal muscle relaxation, extensive perineal stretching, and minimal muscular effort. It also provides the best safeguard against serious perineal tears. When a woman lies on her back, her feet in stirrups, and attempts to push against gravity, a tear is likely to begin in deep tissues beneath the skin's surface. In the supported squatting position, however, any tear will usually be superficial and will quickly heal. Other ways of preventing serious perineal tears are to avoid giving orders ("Push!" "Don't push!"), which are seldom in tune with what the woman feels, and to refrain from pulling on the baby's head for the delivery of the shoulders.

Another reason why episiotomies are so rare at our clinic is that the midwives simply don't like to perform them—which brings up the question of whether this cutting of the vagina reflects some specifically male insensitivity. Naturally, conventional obstetricians have made every attempt to justify their practice. They argue that episiotomies reduce the likelihood of future uterine prolapse,* although there is no scientific evidence to support this hypothesis. In my own surgical experience, I have found that prolapse is

*A condition in which the vaginal muscles, injured or strained during delivery, can no longer support the uterus.

much more likely to occur when doctors accelerate labor artificially, putting a greater strain on the muscles, or deliver with forceps, which may actually damage the muscles. The fact that episiotomies are routine yet generally done without reason makes it even more upsetting to learn that they can cause women pain and sexual problems for weeks afterward. Such complications do not often arise after a natural tear, which heals far more quickly than an episiotomy.

The consequences of our approach are perhaps most strikingly demonstrated in our cesarean rate of 6–7 percent, which stands in provocative contrast to the increasingly high rates throughout the world (19 percent in the United States as of 1982; 13 percent in England, and 15 percent in France). The most famous professor of obstetrics in France recently declared that he thought a 20 percent cesarean rate eminently reasonable. Many explanations are offered for this increase. Doctors, in good faith, attribute it to an increased concern for the safety of the baby. But other factors are involved as well. Although the financial reasons are rarely predominant, in some countries, the operation brings in a great deal of money to private hospitals: in Rio de Janeiro, for example, the cesarean rate is much higher in private hospitals than in public ones, with one private hospital recording a rate of 80 percent! In addition, the danger of lawsuits plays an important part. An obstetrician today is rarely condemned for doing an unnecessary cesarean, but if a baby dies during labor, it is easy to say in retrospect that the operation might have saved it. The simplest way to avoid legal problems is to be absolutely conventional—and, in this respect, we at Pithiviers are very vulnerable. Another contributing factor to the rising cesarean rate is that medical students are not being trained these days to deal with complicated labors such as breech births, or even long normal labors, without resorting to surgery. Once again, conventional medicine seems to treat birth itself as a complication, a pathology calling for intervention. One of the fundamental reasons for the increase in cesareans may well be the deep-seated need of male obstetricians to control the process of childbirth. Certainly the dramatic rise in the cesarean rate (in the United States, from 4.5 per one hundred deliveries in 1965 to 19 in 1982) suggests that cesareans are no longer being used simply as an emergency birth method to save the life of mother and child. Obviously there are reasons for cesarean sections that are indisputable, but these rising frequencies seem increasingly questionable. Unfortunately, the emotional and physical trauma associated with cesarean births which might once have led women to protest has been obscured by custom. Women have become inured to the idea of cesareans precisely because the procedure is now so commonplace—we have arrived at second and third generations of

mothers on whom "medicalized" births have been imposed—and because it is so strongly backed by the medical establishment.

In the rare instances when vaginal delivery is truly unwise or impossible, we, like everyone else, do cesarean sections. For example, we never hesitate to perform a cesarean when the baby presents frontally—with the forehead, instead of the back or top of the head, lying over the cervix—or in a transverse position—when the baby lies sideways in the uterus. We also do one when there is a sudden prolapse of the cord more than five or ten minutes before the probable moment of birth. (Such a compression of the cord is very dangerous, for it will reduce and then suppress the exchange of blood between the baby and the placenta, thereby cutting off the baby's oxygen supply.) A cesarean is also imperative if there is any obstacle in the infant's way, such as a placenta previa that completely covers the cervix. Finally, any unexpected fetal distress can lead to a cesarean.

Obviously, every group of birth attendants will have its own criteria for assessing the risks and indications. It is significant, however, that at Pithiviers, cesareans seem necessary less frequently than elsewhere. The fact is that common hospital procedures, notably absent at our clinic, themselves often create the need for cesareans. The induction of labor by drugs, commonly practiced in Western hospitals, produces more difficult, painful, and protracted labor and is thus frequently the prelude to cesarean section. So is the artificial rupture of the membranes, which may cause a prolapsed umbilical cord. (Conversely, prolapsed cords happen rarely when membranes are not artificially ruptured.) As the fluid in which the umbilical cord floats spills out of the sac of membranes, the cord may drop down before the baby's head and be squeezed or compressed completely, so that the infant's oxygen supply is blocked. Fetal distress results and a cesarean becomes necessary. Drugs that accelerate labor may also interfere with the baby's oxygen supply, since the baby is deprived of oxygen during contractions, and artificial Pitocin-induced contractions are stronger and more frequent than spontaneous ones. The result, again, may be fetal distress and a cesarean.

The pain-relieving drugs often administered to the mother to alleviate her suffering from Pitocin-induced contractions may disturb the process of labor and also lead to cesarean sections. More generally speaking, conventional hospital procedures—the insertion of electronic monitors (which often falsely record fetal distress), the vaginal examinations, the intravenous drips—may all inhibit the woman in labor. Fear stops her labor: a cesarean is judged necessary. It is alarming but true that the more medicine gets involved with childbirth, the more complex and difficult everything becomes. Our low percentage of cesareans at Pithiviers suggests that a practice whose first objective is to help a woman give birth without disturb-

ing the physiological process at any point is the best way of diminishing the number of cesarean sections.

At Pithiviers, we almost never plan cesareans. Even if we suspect that a cesarean will in the end become necessary, we prefer to wait for labor to begin spontaneously, and then depend upon our experience to help us make quick judgments. First of all, since we have reason to believe that the fetal endocrine system plays a role in triggering the onset of labor, when labor begins spontaneously, it means the baby has adequately developed pituitary and adrenal glands and is mature enough to cope with the rigors of labor and birth. Second, it seems that the uterine contractions during labor play a role in stimulating the neuroendocrinological system of the infant, and we do not want to deprive the baby of any part of this stimulation.

Finally, within the realm of labor and birth, one quickly learns to expect the unexpected. Sometimes a woman will have a quick and easy labor when professionals believed only a cesarean was possible. For example, women who have previously had a cesarean are sometimes told that they will always give birth that way. Yet at our clinic, one out of two women who have previously had cesareans succeed in giving birth vaginally. Nor do breech deliveries always justify the operation, although this has, nevertheless, become almost the rule in many conventional hospitals. From our experience with breech babies, we have found that by observing the

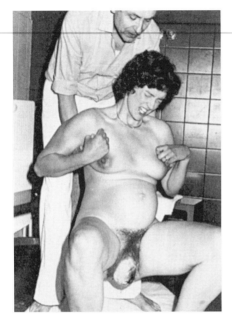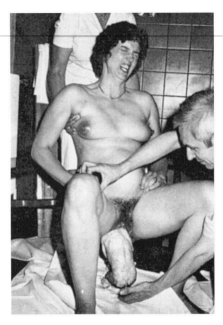

A breech birth in the supported squatting position . . .

natural progression of first-stage labor, we will get the best indication of what to expect at the last moment. This means we do nothing that will interfere with first-stage labor: no Pitocin, no bathing in the pool, no mention of the word "breech." If all goes smoothly, we have reason to believe the second stage of labor will not pose any problems. Our only intervention will be to insist on the supported squatting position for delivery, since it is the most mechanically efficient. It reduces the likelihood of our having to pull the baby out and is the best way to minimize the delay between the delivery of the baby's umbilicus and the baby's head, which could result in the compression of the cord and deprive the infant of oxygen. We would never risk a breech delivery with the mother in a dorsal or semi-seated position.

If, on the other hand, contractions in first-stage labor are painful and inefficient and dilation does not progress, we must quickly dispense with the idea of vaginal delivery. Otherwise we face the danger of a last-minute "point of no return" when, after the emergence of the baby's buttocks, it is too late to switch strategies and decide on a cesarean. However, although we always perform cesareans when first-stage labor is difficult and the situation is not improving, most breech births in our clinic do end up as vaginal deliveries.

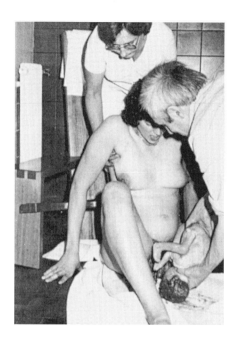
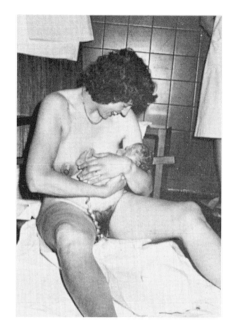
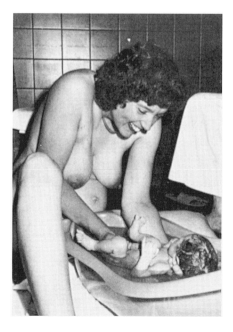
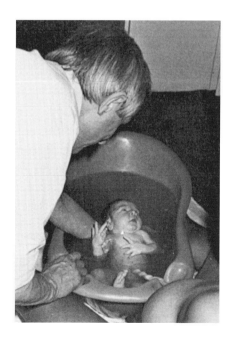

We sometimes plan cesareans in advance in two situations. The first is when the mother develops pre-eclampsia. If a woman has an abrupt increase in blood pressure toward the end of pregnancy and shows protein in her urine, we hospitalize her and watch over her carefully. If she rests on her left side, to relieve the pressure on the vena cava, her blood pressure will sometimes go down and she can then deliver normally. A woman in this state should not take any medication. If she gets sudden headaches and feels as if there is a bar over her stomach, or if the amnioscope shows that the waters are not clear, we will do a cesarean right away. This is the only way to insure that her condition does not develop into eclampsia: convulsions followed by a comatose state that can lead to her death or the baby's. Most cases of pre-eclampsia occur in the last weeks of pregnancy, sometimes appearing during labor itself.

We also occasionally do a cesarean without waiting for labor to begin spontaneously when a pregnancy has gone beyond term. A truly overdue baby is rare, however; there is a common tendency to overestimate the frequency of this happening, usually because the mother or the obstetrician has calculated wrong or is mistaken about the date of conception. When we are certain that a woman is really overdue, we do an amnioscopy every thirty-six hours; as long as the amniotic fluid remains clear, we wait patiently. We see no good reason for routinely inducing labor in such cases with intravenous drips of Pitocin or by breaking the membranes. Perhaps once a year, however, such an amnioscopy reveals colored or diminishing amniotic fluid, and these signs of fetal distress require immediate intervention. If the prospective mother has already had children, perhaps we will rupture the membranes and see what happens before deciding on a cesarean. In the case of a woman having her first baby, we generally expect a longer and more difficult labor, and therefore generally prefer to do a cesarean immediately, so as not to add to the difficulty. With such a strategy, the number of cesareans in connection with "postmaturity" remains very low.

On the whole, cesareans at our clinic remain emergency measures. Our approach significantly lowers the rate of intervention because it means that we do not perform cesareans automatically—only when they are absolutely necessary. And since we generally end up deciding on cesarean section unexpectedly, right before birth, we cannot use any anesthesia that requires long preparation, such as an epidural. We typically use a light general anesthetic that lasts just long enough for the operation, and we operate as quickly as possible. Often the father is present at a cesarean to welcome his baby, and usually the infant is nursing within two hours.

In both vaginal and cesarean deliveries, the hours immediately after birth are also regarded as a possibly dangerous period for mothers and their newborns. Here, too, our philosophy and experience have led us to minimize intervention and, when it is indicated, to choose the least intrusive means.

The baby might have problems breathing just after birth. In most hospitals, it is common practice to introduce a tube into the nose and mouth of every infant right after birth to clear the passages. This is frequently the reason given for the immediate separation of mother and child. At Pithiviers, the newborn is immediately placed in the "safety position": on its stomach, with its head turned to one side. In this position the baby's respiratory tract is protected, even if its reflexes are not yet strong enough for it to cough or cry. There is no danger in waiting patiently for several moments for the mus-

cular tone and reflexes to improve. Then, however, if the infant is still not breathing, we have to clear the airway. For this purpose we use just the funnel-shaped end of a monaural obstetrical stethoscope—the end fits snugly over the baby's mouth and nose—and gently suck the mucus out with our mouths through the funnel. Some infants require short ventilatory assistance with an oxygen mask. After several seconds, the newborn is usually able to breathe on its own and starts to cry. But what if, after a few minutes, the child is still unable to breathe without the help of the oxygen mask? In such exceptional cases, we will then place a tube in the baby's windpipe and rhythmically and gently blow air directly into the lungs. If the newborn continues to have respiratory difficulty, or if there was an excessive amount of

Using the stethoscope to clear the respiratory passages

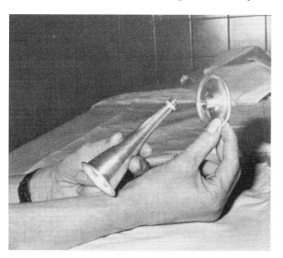 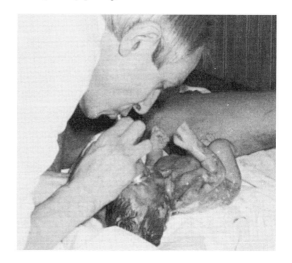

amniotic fluid at birth (which often coincides with respiratory problems), we use a probe to check that the esophagus is unobstructed. One must, finally, consider the possibility that the breathing problem is related to a malformation that can be surgically corrected, such as a blocked esophagus or a diaphragmatic hernia.

The mother's health may also be at risk shortly after birth. In the case of cesarean deliveries, the risks to the mother are statistically more serious than those occasioned by vaginal delivery. In the case of vaginal delivery, if there are any difficulties in the detachment of the placenta or if hemorrhaging begins, immediate action is also required. First we compensate for the blood loss; then we remove the placenta manually and use oxytocic drugs to help the uterus contract. These events occur very seldom at Pithiviers; indeed, they almost never happen when the labor process has been respected all along.

Moreover, we have found that a woman can guard against hemorrhage simply by sitting upright after delivery to welcome her child. When she is in a vertical position, bending slightly forward to hold her baby, her still-heavy uterus does not lie on the vena cava and blood is able to return easily through her veins. Early suckling and skin-to-skin contact between mother and infant can also help to prevent maternal hemorrhage; both processes apparently stimulate the secretion of oxytocin, which in turn causes the uterus to contract, aiding both detachment and expulsion of the placenta. Our 1-percent incidence of manual removal of the placenta speaks strongly in favor of respecting the interrelated physiology of mother and child after delivery. When birth takes place at home, it is even more important to refrain from disturbing this interrelationship of mother and newborn, since hemorrhages are potentially more dangerous outside the hospital.

Our strategy is easy to summarize: we almost always wait for labor to start on its own. If vaginal delivery seems to be difficult, we have three medical techniques at our disposal: Pitocin (rarely); vacuum extraction and episiotomy (sometimes); if delivery by the vaginal route appears impossible or dangerous in any way, we do not hesitate to perform a cesarean.

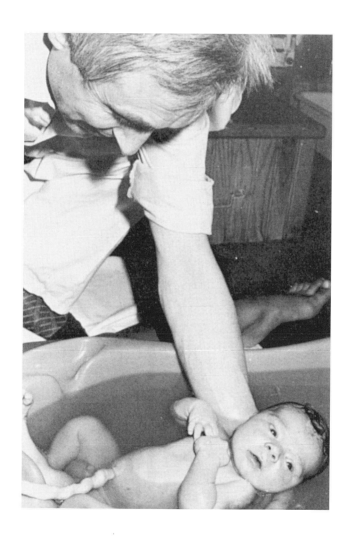

Dominique Pourré, midwife

I came to Pithiviers as a midwife ten years ago, more by instinct than by choice. But I chose to stay. All that I have learned here about women, men, doctors, midwives—and myself—has made it impossible for me to go back to any job that neglects this knowledge, that focuses only on training, internships, examinations. The past ten years have taught me one very important thing: women must be careful not to place themselves so totally in the hands of doctors and midwives when giving birth to their children. As professionals, we have been trained to be cool, distant, technical—and yet we can do no wrong in their eyes. How,

then, can we not continue to believe, and to make others believe, that women, within this domain of childbirth, lack creativity and incentive, that they await our solutions? We act for them, we teach them, we organize their entire lives, even their emotions, at these crucial moments. It was to this training, these attitudes, the continual reinforcement of this authority and hierarchy that my decade at Pithiviers has presented a sustained and triumphant challenge.

Michel Odent's basic idea for mothers was this: "Don't follow someone else's advice. No one knows better than you what is right for your baby." The prospective mother was now responsible for what could become a joyous occasion. Instead of letting someone else deliver her child, comfort it, or give the first bath, it was up to her to take part, to do it herself.

I had just had a son myself, and perhaps this made me more sensitive to these truths. I soon decided that, despite the traditional prerogatives of my role as midwife, I could no longer be the first to touch the baby. I would not, any more, whisk the newborn into another room, for some mysterious reason I've long forgotten. I would stop wearing rubber gloves, so that the infant's first contact would be with human skin. It wasn't easy, but I was trying. And I would let the child be caressed

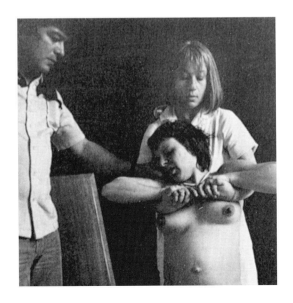

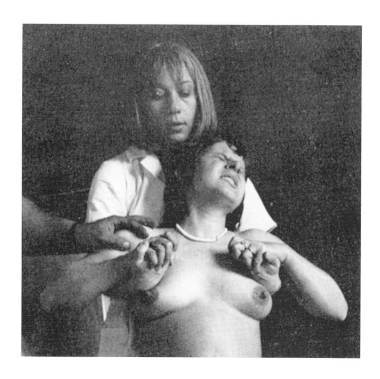

by its mother. Yes, I say "let," for we professionals still kept the power; we still gave the green light for the liberation and expression of emotions —or, more frequently, as convention and routine had taught us, the red light.

Mothers had to start taking the initiative. They could no longer fear the fragile, slippery feel of their babies. We had to say to them: "You can deliver the baby yourself. Reach out and grasp those tiny arms, they are reaching for you. Don't be afraid, you can do it. It's your baby." Not ours,

not the doctors', not some strange product of medical knowledge, technique, or power. But it wasn't as simple as it sounds.

You don't give up the professionally sanctioned role of "baby-snatcher" without a great deal of self-denial. When I was the official "snatcher," I was so relieved by the sight of the baby; I would think: "That's it, a baby boy, here he is, alive! I can hold him, I have the right. Oh, I was so scared he might not exist. Yes, just like you, the mother. I had the same feelings, the same anxiety. And now

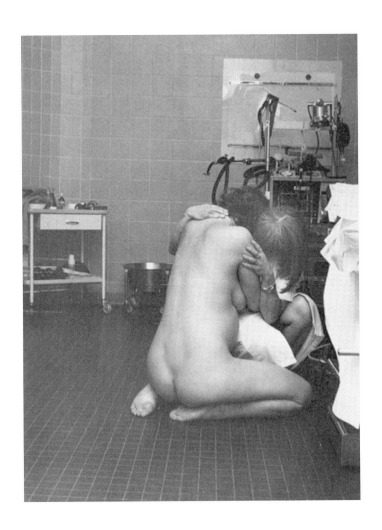

I'll give you a present: your child. But first I have to examine him, bathe him, weigh him, dress him." There seemed to be no end to the extent to which a baby could belong to someone other than its mother. And these baby-snatchers, dressed in white, these mysterious figures who talked out loud and made the decisions—what were we hiding behind our gauze masks? Fear of death, fear of women? Can't we find another way? Are we really so reassuring? How can women actually believe that we know more about these things than they do?

So now, take off the masks! Let the roles be reversed!

I'm here, I'm listening to you. What are you feeling? I can help you if you tell me what you want. Talk to me. Teach me. I don't want to stand in front of you any more, active and powerful.

Today at Pithiviers, I can sit back, listen, be part of an intimate act. The woman is standing. She lets me know what's going on: that she feels changes in her body; that she wants to push; that she has to open a bit more; that the membranes full of waters are bulging between her fingers. She tells me what she wants: warmth; hot water; her husband's caresses, or maybe my own. She expresses her feelings: how much it hurts; that she wants the student nurses with their wide eyes to leave the room because they are stopping up something inside her; that I'm not always as soft and gentle as she would like me to be; that she wants it to be over; that she wants to scream; that she is going to do it. I hear her as she cries out, and I no longer try to quiet her. She becomes my teacher. I listen to her, I study her lessons. I myself am also pregnant, pregnant with her words, her pains, her strange cries which even she does not recognize as her own.

I am overcome. There is nothing to teach her. She pushes for life on her own. I am not to touch her. She shouts at me: "Stay back. I am giving birth. Leave me alone!" She makes herself comfortable, and I must accommodate myself to her position. She moves around. She is creative, inventive, full of life. She looks for what she wants. She is exhausted and yet so vital. As she throws herself upon me, I am covered in her sweat. I am obliged to do as she wishes. But she is beautiful, she is the life that she is about to bring forth. She no longer asks me the time, the sex, the weight. Instead, she simply cries out with pleasure. I leave the room, exhausted, full of her emotions, her joy.

In ten years at Pithiviers, I have been taught: where women are free, we will learn how they give birth best. They will show us. They will trust us. Look at them. Listen closely .

Meeting-room mural painted by the father of a baby born at Pithiviers

birth reborn

During a panel game show on French radio one day, the contestants were asked the following question: "What is special about childbirth at Pithiviers?" It was not an easy question. Even I would have had trouble choosing the proper one-line response. As it turned out, the "correct" answer was: "Women give birth in a squatting position." Fair enough, but there were plenty of other possible answers: the prominent role of midwives; prolonged contact between mother and child; baths for newborns; singing groups; dim lights; music; pools of warm water for relaxation.

But Pithiviers is more than the sum of its parts. It represents an attitude, a belief in the instinctive potential of human beings and in the innate knowledge women bring to childbirth. Pithiviers affirms birth as a sexual experience, and encourages spontaneity and, above all, freedom. A pregnant woman is free to visit our maternity unit as often or as seldom as she likes. She is free to reject any form of preparation that pretends to "teach"

her how to give birth. She is free to move as she wishes during labor. Couples are free to act as they please in the privacy of the birthing room.

The introduction of freedom into an institution is neither an easy nor a trivial accomplishment. In fact, the concepts "freedom" and "institution" seem by definition incompatible. Yet as our experience has shown, more can be done than is usually even attempted. Ideally, institutions can actually offer a sense of community.

In our efforts to create freedom in the birth environment, we are continually questioning our roles as professionals. Professionals in general and representatives of the medical community in particular often inhibit the behavior of soon-to-be-parents much more than the average layperson would. At Pithiviers we try to be as discreet as possible, keeping out of the way, staying in the background, simply making sure that nothing abnormal occurs. Although our methods and philosophy challenge prevalent obstetrical assumptions and practices, we find that, measured even by traditional obstetrical standards such as perinatal and maternal morbidity and mortality rates, Pithiviers is a success. For instance, from January 15, 1982, to June 30, 1983, out of 1,402 births, there were 93 cesarean sections (6.6 percent), 73 vacuum extractions (5.2 percent), 84 episiotomies (6 percent), 13 manual removals of the placenta (0.9 percent), 10 perinatal deaths (7.1 per thousand), and 22 infants separated from their mothers (1.5 percent) in order to be transferred to a pediatric or intensive care unit.

Over the last decade, Pithiviers has grown from a traditional provincial maternity unit to something of an international childbirth center, a focal point for the new consciousness of the importance of changing birth conditions. The idea of humanizing childbirth had been gathering force not only at Pithiviers, but also in many different places around the world. Often these small, isolated centers of innovation focused on the personal, rather than the technical or medical, aspects of childbirth. They involved people outside the mainstream of Western medicine who felt the need for a more holistic and spiritual approach to well-being; and those interested in the therapeutic possibilities of touch, sound, music, light, color, and water. Anthropologists, psychotherapists, sociologists, ecologists, and childbirth educators also joined in. At the same time, midwives and pediatricians around the world were de-

manding a heightened awareness of the true needs of mothers and newborns, and calling attention to how these needs had been ignored or forgotten by the medical establishment. Outside of professional circles, consumer advocates and concerned men and women were questioning conventional medical birthing attitudes and practices and struggling to change them.

Today these different groups are communicating more and more with one another. In spite of the geographical distances between them, they have created a powerful worldwide network, linking pioneers in the new obstetrics in Europe, North America, Latin America, New Zealand, Australia, and Japan. Pithiviers has played a major role in the development of this international network and continues to be a key focus. Over the past ten years, parents, midwives, health care professionals, and proponents of alternative medicine from all over the world have gathered at Pithiviers to talk about their work and share their ideas. Television crews and journalists from France, Germany, Great Britain, Australia, and Japan have all come to the clinic to film and interview us and the women giving birth here. It seems to be one of Pithiviers' basic tasks to act as catalyst of an exciting new awareness, and the constant flow of friends and visitors helps us spread the word.

This new consciousness, however, is not without its own internal dilemmas. For example, how do we reconcile the paradox inherent in relying on science and medical professionals to help us rediscover and support women's natural capacities or the natural bonding process between infants and their mothers? What is a man's proper role in a movement that seeks to return the childbirth experience to women? These are questions that trouble me. Presently I am seriously considering leaving obstetrics; this is at a time when male obstetricians would do well to retire progressively and restore childbirth to women.

The chronic obstetrical crisis that has been building for several centuries has now reached an acute stage. The revolution so many of us are seeking will not be triggered by the professionals of obstetrics, or even by the medical professions overall. Not that science and medicine will have no future contributions to make. In years to come, for example, it is likely that technical advances will make it possible for non-invasive, wireless fetal monitoring to be used, so that there will be no more excuse to disturb the birth process in order to gain essential informa-

tion. Progress in scientific disciplines, such as neurophysiology, despite their apparent distance from obstetrics, may also contribute to this revolution. I believe that the nature of labor and delivery will be increasingly understood as an involuntary brain process that may profitably be studied by those concerned with physiological changes of consciousness, such as sleep and orgasm. But the most powerful movers of this revolution will be women themselves.

How women give birth and how children are born are profoundly tied to our views of nature, science, health, medicine, freedom, and human—especially man-woman—relationships. Our ambitious project, which struggles to humanize and feminize birth, uses very simple means to achieve this end. In fact, the local women who have given birth at our clinic refer to our style of doing things as plain common sense. These women find our attitude so obvious that they can't imagine what so many visitors and film crews are doing here. Their astonishment is worth thinking about.